JOHN WESTLEY CLAYTON PRESENTS...

GOD
IN BUSINESS

FAITH IS THE
DECIDING FACTOR

Cover Photo Credit:
ShutterStock photo ID: 262210673
By Khakimullin Aleksandr
Businessman goes straight on his way on asphalt road

Table of Contents

Dedication

This book is dedicated to all of the men and women of faith who boldly allow God to work through them in their workplace without putting a bushel over their Lamp.

Acknowledgements

I'd like to first give thanks to our Lord and Savior Jesus Christ for His gift of Grace and salvation through Faith in Him. Without Him none of this is possible.

Thank you to all the faithful authors who dedicated their precious time and talents to contributing to this project. Valen Vergara, Donna & Steve Coplon, Deana Mitchell, Taft Mohair II, Geoff Hudson-Searle, Rudy Lira Kusuma, Chuck Bolena, Kevin V. Riles, Mark H. Tekamp, Scott McGregor and Ken Bitkowski.

Thank you to my incredibly talented cover designer Brad Szollose.

Foreword

Professionally, I've led, mentored and served thousands of military members and their families during my more than 30 years in the United States Air Force. Since retiring from the military, I served as the program director for a geriatric mental health program that served a diverse and important population. The Director of Health Services for the SC Department of Corrections and was responsible for 650 medical professionals and serve our 22 thousand patients across the state of South Carolina, and am currently the Director, Support Services City of Sumter. I have been recognized as a bestselling Author three times. With all those accolades, one would think that I have always lived a charmed and successful life. That my friends; has not been the case. In March of 1986 I very nearly lost myself. As that great book the *Tale of Two Cities* posited, it was the best of times and the worst of times. On March 18th my first son was born but on March 4th my favorite person Annie Mae Fate died; she was my heart and also my mother. It was a very tough time for me because I couldn't be happy about my son because I was grieving and I couldn't properly grieve because I was trying to celebrate the birth of my son. I was pretty messed up. I was angry at everyone, My Mom, My Wife, My Boss, My Son, Myself and My God! I was drifting and I was lost. What saved me was a great supervisor by the name of John Gunther. He was a great man and a great military leader; he was also a believer in Christ. He had the opportunity to let me self-destruct but he chose to help me. He was a leader and learner and he reintroduced me to study. Two books were on him all the time; *Bible* and *Think and Grow Rich*. I started following his lead and doing what I saw him doing. He didn't only read but he lived what he was reading. I saw in him what I wanted to be and that was an unapologetic believer in God, and someone who studied and worked hard to be successful. He didn't just do it in his personal life and on Sunday but he lived his truth 24/7, 365 days of the year. He brought his faith with him to work and he lived his faith.

There have been times in my life and in my career where I tried to live apart from my faith and to keep those parts of my life separate. These times were where I struggled most. Sergeant Gunther taught me to live in integrity. To live in integrity is to be as one in all facets of life.

1 Corinthians 10:31

"Whether therefore ye eat, or drink, or whatsoever ye do, do all to the glory of God."

Colossians 3:17

"And whatsoever ye do in word or deed, do all in the name of the Lord Jesus, giving thanks to God and the Father by him."

As a Retired Command Chief Master Sergeant, I have had some of the best training and have served with some of the best leaders that our country has to offer. The best lesson I have ever learned is to live your faith, not just talk about it. I am honored to be a part of this body of work on *"God In Business"* because it shows us how to live our faith. This book will walk you through ways in which you can keep God in all parts of your life, not just your church walk. When we focus on Him first, all parts of our lives will be in order. This book and the stories in it will be a light to your path and a lamp to your feet.

Be blessed my friends; and go with God.

Lefford Fate

A Word From The Publisher

I didn't grow up in a Christian family. As a matter of fact, it was probably quite the opposite. My parents brought us to church every so often just as a feel-good gesture. I knew noting about Jesus. It wasn't till about 1991 that I started to attend a church regularly, only because I thought it was the right thing to do since my first daughter was born. That's what you do, right? When you have kids, you bring them to church. It didn't really matter to me what church was for; just go.

Well, in 1992 my life would change forever. I was attending a small Baptist Church and heard of a play called *"Heavens Gates and Hell's Flames"* that was playing at the Baptist Church down the road. I decided to go. What would it hurt, right? Watch a play, go home, back to life as usual. Not so much.

This play was a reenactment of the lives of believers and non-believers; during their lives and at the moment they died and faced Jesus at their judgement. I've heard things about sin, judgement, Jesus paying the price, etc. but never really put much thought into it. It *"just wasn't me"*, as people say. At the end, the pastor made an alter call for anyone who wanted to have their sins forgiven and make Jesus the Lord of their life.

It was at that moment that I saw a need for a savior. I had been a sinner my whole life and my sins needed to be paid for. With tears rolling down my face, I went up to the alter and surrendered my life to Jesus. I asked him to forgive my sins and be the Lord of my life.

I was on FIRE!!! I thought for sure God wanted me to be a pastor. Right away I went to the New Orleans Baptist Theological Seminary to enroll. I did not get in. Some may take this as a "*sign*" that I am not supposed to be in ministry, just as I did.

It wasn't till many years later that I learned that all Christians are supposed to be in ministry in some capacity, even if not in the church. We are ministers of our Lord every day of the week and in every area of our life. We must let the Light shine through our life. So many people are Christians at church, but there's no evidence at home or at work.

"What if the church on Sunday
Was still the church on Monday too?"
Band-Casting Crowns
Song-Start Right Here
Album-Only Jesus

God gave me the idea of publishing this book on this subject about two years ago. The seed was planted, but the soil wasn't ready. The time has come.

The purpose of this book and the stories in it is to inspire Christians to live out their Christian lives in all areas of their life, personally and professionally. Also, to inspire non-Christians to seek Jesus to be their Lord and Savior.

Revelation 3:15-16 (NKJV)

[15] *"I know your works, that you are neither cold nor hot. I could wish you were cold or hot.* [16] *So then, because you are lukewarm, and neither [a]cold nor hot, I will vomit you out of My mouth."*

As you read, I pray that you can hear the voices of the authors and feel what they felt as they wrote it. I know tears were shed in the process, including mine. I purposely did very little editing for this very reason. Each chapter is in the author's own words.

Thank you and God Bless you
John Westley Clayton

CHAPTER I

Faith, Friends, Finance

By Valen Vergara

FORTUNE FAVOURS THE BOLD!

This chapter is steadfast to mentorship, empowerment, and development of the faculty of faith. To bring about the bumping of every area of business into a higher bracket. In an effort to permeate ideas that are dedicated to improving lives, enhancing hearts, and strengthening minds. Become bolstered by boldness. Let go and let God!

My vivid mission is to connect, coexist, and contribute to a diverse group of high yielding individuals, non-profits, international organizations, foundations, and initiatives that enrich believers to manifest their statements of belief.

Embedded in this section are three topics that will teach you how to push past your own obstructions. This is for the movers and shakers, those based in faith, and for those who are beholden to no one but God.

FAITH

Suspending disbelief is easier said than done. Taking action with unknowns in our midst is a feat that many shy away from. If the initiation of faith is idled the battle going on inside with our mindset will be lost before it has begun. Unknowingly, we can end up becoming our own worst enemy.

Such activation energy governs the collective consciousness of humanity. When we come up with an idea that we desire to transition into action it usually takes about five seconds or so for our enthusiasm to wane due to a compilation of excuses. The time we spend inside these critical seconds of inspired imagination is when we need to take stock of said blockages.

Act wisely!

A war wages on to weaken our resolve, thwart our wherewithal, and to usurp the throne for our train of thought. We must not allow absentmindedness, nor one word or sentence, to invade the sanctity of our state of mind. We tend to say about three hundred to four hundred words per minute to ourselves. We need to think about what we are thinking about and get out of our own way!

An idea penned down with a due date becomes an agreement. An objective broken down becomes a blueprint. A blueprint backed by action steps becomes a movement. Employ these three actions steps and excellence will prevail.

God has a lot in store for us!

Eighty percent of faith is showing up. Eighty-five percent of it is showing up at the right time. Ninety percent of it is showing up on time with a plan. Ninety-five percent of it is showing up on time, with a plan, and implementing properly. This allows for one hundred percent of the chances for opportunity.

Focus is following one course until successful. On average, we lose focus every six seconds. In order to do so, we must come to the conclusion that time is not more important than our attention.

Time waits for no one!

Concentration is in concert with how we conduct success. It dictates our hopes and dreams and everything in between. Thoughts generate gravity and the way you think alters your reality. If you spend too much time thinking about what you do not have and how you are not getting what you want, you will continue to attract just that, and that is lack. What we focus on expands, the good, and the bad. As the Bible said best, *"As a man thinketh in his heart, so is he!"*

"A man who went through a near death experience. During his time spent on the other side, the man had a face-to-face conversation with the devil himself. It was in that moment in time that the man asked this question, 'What is your greatest weapon against humankind?' The devil's smile seemed to make his cheeks hurt as he pulled a wedge out from under him and said, 'Do you see this wedge? I call it The Wedge of Doubt. If I can thrust this wedge into your consciousness, I can separate you from your faith, and divide and conquer you'!"

— The Wedge of Doubt

James 2:18-24

¹⁸ *But someone will say, "You have faith; I have deeds." Show me your faith without deeds, and I will show you my faith by my deeds.*
¹⁹ *You believe that there is one God. Good! Even the demons believe that—and shudder.*
²⁰ *You foolish person, do you want evidence that faith without deeds is useless?*
²¹ *Was not our father Abraham considered righteous for what he did when he offered his son Isaac on the altar?*
²² *You see that his faith and his actions were working together, and his faith was made complete by what he did.*
²³ *And the scripture was fulfilled that says, "Abraham believed God, and it was credited to him as righteousness," and he was called God's friend.*
²⁴ *You see that a person is considered righteous by what they do and not by faith alone.*

FRIENDS

We are the average of our five closest associations. As it has been said before, *"Birds of a feather flock together."* We eat, sleep, earn, yearn, and learn just like the individuals we let into our lives. Jesus carefully hand selected his disciples. The first two were brothers and fishermen, and the next two were friends of the brothers and fishermen as well.

Teamwork makes the dream work!

People are the most powerful, influential resource on planet Earth. The four main aspects of trade are goods, services, people, and ideas. Every day of existence we *"sell"* one another on products, services, and ideas all around the world.

Ideas turn into information. Information is made up of pieces of data. More data is being created in the year of this publication than in all the previous years combined. This data is continuing to be made at an unprecedented rate and it is being exchanged from peer to peer.

There is limitless potential when we become impregnated with useful information. Insight can be conceived by a single piece of advice. This gives birth to a new direction and it cries out to be delivered by your decision to raise it into action! On the other hand, there are adverse effects that can take place when we are poisoned with harmful information.

Be careful who you listen to!

According to Albert Einstein and Thomas Edison:

"The human brain emits a frequency which when focused, is picked up by other human brains, and this affects physical matter. It passes through the ether, through solid objects, and travels faster than the speed of light. There is a magnetic pull."

What we are looking for is already trying to catch us because the frequencies match; whether it be negative or positive. Our level of vibration is low or high and is noticeable by others. If it is low it is *"pessimistic,"* if it is high it is *"optimistic."* Filter out things that do not work in your favour.

"Socrates was reputed to hold knowledge in high esteem. One day, an acquaintance met the great philosopher and said, "Do you know what I heard about that person?"

"Hold on a minute", Socrates replied. "Before telling me anything I'd like you to pass a little test. It's called the Triple Filter Test."

"Triple filter?"

"That's right", Socrates continued. "Before you talk to me about that person, it might be a good idea to take a moment and filter what you're going to say. That's why I call it the triple filter test.

The first filter is Truth. Have you made absolutely sure that what you are about to tell me is true?"

"No," the man said, "Actually I just heard about it..."

"All right", said Socrates. "So, you don't really know if it's true or not.

*Now, let's try the second filter, the filter of
Goodness. Is what you are about to tell me about
that person something good?"*

"No, on the contrary."

*"So", Socrates continued, "you want to tell me
something bad about that person, but you're not
certain if it's true.*

*You may still pass the test though, because there's
one filter left: the filter of Usefulness. Is what
you want to tell me about that person going to
be useful to me?"*

"No, not really."

*"Well", concluded Socrates, "if what you want to
tell me about this person is neither true, nor
good, nor even useful, why tell it to me at all?"*

Like the saying goes, *"A chain is only as strong as the weakest
link."* A friend can also turn out to be a foe. Judas Iscariot kissed
Jesus in the Garden of Gethsemane right before betraying him.
Unfortunately for us, our response to the same situation in our life
is, *"I did not see that coming!"*

Choose wisely!

United we stand, divided we fall.

Ecclesiastes 4:12

*¹² And if one prevaileth against him,
two shall withstand him; and a
three-fold cord is not quickly broken.*

FINANCE

Where did the main idea of money come from?

It came from Europe and from a group of salespeople called the *"Money Changers."* Jesus drove these sellers out from the temple. It was the only time Jesus used force during his ministry.

When Jews came to Jerusalem to pay the temple tax, they could only pay it with a special coin the *"Half Shekel of the Sanctuary."* (A half-ounce of pure silver). It was the only coin around at that time which was pure silver of an assured weight without an image of a pagan emperor.

Therefore, to the Jews this coin was the only coin acceptable to God. These coins were not plentiful, and these money managers cornered the market. They raised the price just like any other commodity to as much as the market could bear. These investors were making incredible profits because they held a monopoly on money. The Jews had to pay whatever they demanded. To Jesus this totally violated the sanctity of Gods house.

It is in our nature to fear what we do not understand! Can we really decipher something we have not defined? No! If we fail to do so, we are bounded by misinformation! Liberation is found through definition.

What is money?

The economic definition of money is something that serves as a medium of exchange, a unit of accounting, and a store of value, that we all agree to accept in making transactions!

Money is a mirror that reflects our moral character. It is a symbolic transaction. It has no intrinsic value; it is extrinsic. The only meaning it has is the meaning we attach to it. Money is a merely a reflection of our moral fiber. It is an amplifier. It makes us more of who we already are. It is only a carbon copy of our inner game at play.

It is communication between two value forms. Most users misinterpret money. They do not see the value in it. They value it!; instead of the value it represents! It is not the love of money that is truly the root of all evil. It is the misunderstanding of it that is.

Money is just an instrument; there is no need to fall victim to it.

Invest wisely!

Matthew 21:12-13

[12] Jesus entered the temple courts and drove out all who were buying and selling there. He overturned the tables of the moneychangers and the benches of those selling doves.
[13] "It is written," he said to them, "My house will be called a house of prayer,' but you are making it 'a den of robbers.'"

Valen Vergara | Bio

Chairman of WEPT, Corp., focus on acquisitions, business development, banking, energy, financing, fine arts, forex, infrastructure, large-cap projects, management, and real estate.

Chief Operations Officer and director at Aureum Energy Corporation. Aureum Energy is key to the future of provision of clean solutions to the globe by solving one of its greatest issues - plastic pollution.

President and Founder of Team Made Real Estate, Inc. (TMR), an online real estate investing academy and one of the top-rated real estate education networks in Canada. CEO of Team Made Developments, the private equity real estate investment sector. Owner at Team Made Properties, property management sector. Owner at Team Made Construction, renovations sector.

Co-Founder of Culture Card, Inc. Culture Card received recognition for a creative and innovative marketing campaign that increases visitation by Winnipeg Tourism.

Founder of The Worldwide Expedition for Peace and Truth Project, Inc. (WEPT). The project subscribes to sustainable philanthropy by fundraising for humanitarian campaigns.

CHAPTER II

Raising Godly Children: God In The Workplace Starts At Home

By Donna & Steve Coplon

Deuteronomy 6:4-7 NIV

4 Hear, O Israel: The LORD
our God, the LORD is one.
5 Love the LORD your God with all your
heart and with all your soul
and with all your strength.
6 These commandments that I give you today
are to be on your hearts.
7 Impress them on your children.

What a blessing it is to share some of my thoughts, ideas, and experiences with others to help all of us to live a more healthy and happy life, especially when dealing with the different relationships in our lives. Relationships at home in our families and in the workplace, all begin with a word that seems to have lost its meaning in our homes and communities more than ever, that word is respect. Respect has to be taught and it starts in the home.

When a child is born and then begins to crawl for the first time, they learn very quickly what they are allowed to touch and not touch. As they grow, they learn that their hands are for holding and exploring, not for hitting one another. This is the first lesson in teaching respect to our little ones. As they go through the toddler years, they interact with others by learning to share and learning to speak with kind words. They learn everything by listening to the way the parents speak. Using words like thank you, please, and you're welcome. They listen to our tone; they watch our expressions. This teaches them attitude and response. As good manners are being taught, patience is being taught by giving them time in between to receive their food or having them wait a few minutes when taking them out of the car seat. Just by waiting they are learning respect for mom and dad until they can do for themselves.

It is very important to teach a toddler how to respect the home that he or she lives in. I had a friend who totally cleared her items off of all end tables and never put a Christmas tree up until her children were older to avoid them from damaging things.

Instead of teaching her children to respect and don't touch Mommy's things, they used the tables and end tables to climb on.

Raising Godly Children:
God In The Workplace Starts At Home

That's what they did when they came to my house! They didn't understand how to properly behave inside someone else's home.

As children begin learning these things at home, when it's time to start school, they understand how to listen and wait, respect the teacher and other's property, get along with their classmates and how to make friends. Even as young children they have already learned consideration, kindness, patience and thoughtfulness. Talk to our children with kindness and they will respond back in kindness.

Proverbs 22:6 NIV

⁶ Start children off on
the way they should go,
and even when they are old,
they will not turn from it.

I grew up with two sisters; one very close in age and the other, seven years younger. My dad was very kind and very protective over his girls. We went to church every Sunday and were involved in church activities during the week. Our world was school, church and playing community sports.

We always had dinner together as a family. My mother didn't work and always had great meals at night. My dad was very strict about table manners. My mom called us to dinner only once,

31

and we came. Whatever was prepared, we ate, no options. We were told to sit up straight, no slouching. Tie our hair back (we had very long straight hair). We said a blessing over the food. Conversation was light and quiet at the table. One at a time we were allowed to talk. We were told not to talk with our mouths full and no singing. Not to get up until our meal was over. After we ate, we asked to be excused and we were allowed to leave the table. This was just the way it was every night. My dad especially pushed good manners. When company came over, we greeted them and then went and played. My mom and dad were good, fair, loving parents. We never felt like they were too strict. To this day, it is important to all of us to greet people and be respectful to others. These teachings done in the proper way are crucial to becoming a respectful person.

Children have to feel like they're part of a family connection. Respecting their parents and siblings is crucial to how they later treat others outside the home. If children are used to not listening, not talking things over with their parents, not caring about what their brother or sister is doing, only focused on themselves and their own needs, they will continue that life pattern when they leave home. The Bible teaches us to love one another. Loving others cannot be done unless we love God first, then he gives us the power to love others. How can we get along with schoolmates, other employees at work, family members, if you don't have love, which really starts with loving yourself and respecting yourself?

Raising Godly Children:
God In The Workplace Starts At Home

Matthew 22:36-40 NIV

[36] "Teacher, which is the greatest
commandment in the Law?"
[37] Jesus replied: "'Love the Lord your God with
all your heart and with all your soul
and with all your mind.'
[38] This is the first and greatest commandment.
[39] And the second is like it:
'Love your neighbor as yourself.'
[40] All the Law and the Prophets
hang on these two commandments."

Having respect in the home has to be a family effort. I understand that there are different kinds of families. There may not be both parents in the home. It could be a single parent, but no matter what the environment, everyone can learn how to respect one another. As children get older it is crucial that they feel valued and heard. If feelings and emotions never get expressed because of no one listening to them, it could cause loneliness, sadness, and disrespect, not caring about themselves or anyone else. Our job as parents is to prepare our children for adulthood, to be stable, live responsibly on their own and respect themselves enough to be able to respect others.

1 Corinthians 13:4-7 NIV

⁴ Love is patient, love is kind.
It does not envy, it does not
boast, it is not proud.
⁵ It does not dishonor others, it is not self-
seeking, it is not easily angered,
it keeps no record of wrongs.
⁶ Love does not delight in evil
but rejoices with the truth.
⁷ It always protects, always trusts,
always hopes, always perseveres.

When you find your family is not uniting together, most of the time, it's because something is out of balance. It could be too many activities going on; everyone just looking out for themselves and their own needs. No one is getting along. Unfortunately, because of divorce some of my attention wasn't as focused on my children's emotional needs and life values as it should have been. I regret some of the decisions that were made back then which mostly affected my son. He was quiet and never complained about anything. He usually went along with whatever was going on. I missed some major red flags with him during those teen years.

As I look at my life, I could have done so many things differently. I could have made better decisions, listened to God instead of running ahead of him. I guess that's what life is all about - to learn from your mistakes and to help others, not make the same mistakes.

Proverbs 3:5-6 NIV

⁵ Trust in the LORD with all your heart
and lean not on your own understanding;
⁶ in all your ways acknowledge him,
and he will make your paths straight.

We must communicate a real interest in what goes on in the lives of our children as they are growing up and even when they are grown. They must feel like we hear them and accept them no matter what they say or do.

It's so easy to halfway listen when they are speaking. In the early years of raising children, we may find that we are trying to figure out what we want. We may be dealing with financial problems, working a lot and not having time to just sit for a moment. But no matter what, we have to make them feel the unconditional love from us, which we get from our heavenly father.

When they can't count on us to be there for them, they will look somewhere else for love and for acceptance. That's when their lives can go in the wrong direction. Our children should feel like there is *"no place like home"* not *"I don't want to be home."*

They must have discipline and boundaries to live by. We must be specific and consistent. They respect us more as their parents when they know exactly what we expect from them. Remember, if you let a teenager have too much freedom too early, it's hard to reel them back in. This is even true with what you let them watch on TV and movies. They have to be exposed little by little, age appropriate. There's a reason you don't want your child seeing action or killing movies too young because they can become desensitized to violence.

Unfortunately, the world today is exposing our little ones to too much too soon. It's up to parents to moderate their own children even if the world sees nothing wrong with it. Our young children don't know any better, so they aren't the ones that should decide what to watch, eat or wear. That's our job.

As responsible parents we are to provide and meet their material needs - proper clothes, good healthy food, and of course a safe place to live. They have to be taught the difference between wants and needs. At times it gets hard financially. We must pray together as a family for direction and guidance and have faith in God's promises.

Raising Godly Children:
God In The Workplace Starts At Home

Passing on our faith to our children is our responsibility. Our ability to influence our children is tied into their respect for us. We must be parents worthy of the respect of others.

Psalm 27:14 NIV

14 Wait for the LORD;
be strong and take heart
and wait for the LORD.

We as parents must bring up our children to be respectful and respected. It is to love them, accept them, provide for them, and set limits and boundaries for them. And of course, be there for them; always be present.

Titus 2:7 GNT

7 In all things you yourself must be an example
of good behavior. Be sincere and
serious in your teaching.

With all that a parent must teach their children to be Godly in their lives, without teaching them forgiveness, they can never experience peace and contentment. We must have a forgiving heart. Holding unforgiveness and grudges against someone is deadly to our well-being. To be a healthy person inside & out, you have to let go of past mistakes, unfairness and untruthfulness; that involves always forgiving ourselves first from anything we might have done to hurt someone as we accept ourselves and stop feeling shame or blame. We can move on to forgive others that have betrayed us, been unfair, unkind, ignored us and see them as people that are searching for their own truth themselves. If we are able to forgive someone the instant that they offend us, we are better off in the long run. The power of the Holy Spirit is the only way this can be done, not in our own strength.

And the voice of truth says,
"This is for My glory"
Out of all the voices calling out to me
I will choose to listen and believe
the voice of truth
Because Jesus you are the voice of truth
And I will listen to you
Casting Crowns – Voice of Truth

Raising Godly Children:
God In The Workplace Starts At Home

So many voices in the world; I choose to listen to the Voice of Truth, the Word of God.

Well, there you have it. Donna has just laid out, completely from her loving caring heart, what it takes for parents to raise Godly children. As we raise our children and prepare them to go out into the world to take responsibility for themselves and their families, it is my fervent prayer that the lessons that Donna has shared are part of each of our very core being.

Possessing the qualities of being a Godly person that Donna has written about – self-respect, respect for others, respect for others' property, patience, caring, speaking with kind words, thoughtfulness, sharing, listening, politeness, being considerate, showing an interest in others, expressing oneself, truthfulness, proper behavior, and above all else being obedient and waiting on the Lord, will equip you for a life in the workplace, no matter what your career or vocation, that will be filled with peace and harmony. You will be well on the road to success in terms of fulfillment and taking care of responsibility. You will be a valuable member of any team, organization or company.

We need not worry about whether or not we will be able to support our families. We know that the Lord will provide the opportunity to earn the provision that we need to support our families.

Donna & Steve Coplon

Philippians 4:19 NIV

*¹⁹ And my God will meet all your
needs according to the riches of
his glory in Christ Jesus.*

If we have been raised as Godly children, then we should not live separate un-Godly lives at our workplace. We should be the same child of God as we are in our homes and in our churches. Our workplace should be an extension of our families, as we are all brothers and sisters in Christ.

Hebrews 13:8 NIV

*⁸ Jesus Christ is the same yesterday
and today and forever.*

Many times, we take our problems from home to work with us and cannot give a good day's work to our employer. Many times, we take our problems from our workplace home with us and disrupt the peace and harmony of our homes. If we can stay close to God at all times, we will not fall prey to these situations.

Raising Godly Children:
God In The Workplace Starts At Home

Colossians 3:23 NIV

*23 Whatever you do, work at it with all your
heart, as working for the Lord,
not for human masters.*

When we stay close to God in prayer and obedience, we can be a person in our workplace that others seek to be near. Even non-believers will desire our presence. We can be a light to others, as the Holy Spirit works through us as we love others as Christ loves us.

Matthew 5:16 NIV

*16 In the same way, let your light shine before
others, that they may see your good deeds
and glorify your Father in heaven.*

As we raise our children to go into the world and have the life that God wants them to have, we must ask ourselves *"What is it that God really wants for us?"* Donna and I believe that God ultimately only wants us to glorify Him and to have a closer, deeper personal relationship with Him.

Donna & Steve Coplon

Romans 8:28 NIV

²⁸ And we know that in all things God works for the good of those who love him, who have been called according to his purpose.

God Bless you as you raise your children to be Godly and as you yourself draw closer to God.

Steve & Donna Coplon | Bio

Donna and Steve have been called by God to spread their message of Love, Hope and Encouragement to hardship populations.

Steve is the Founder/Executive Director of Right Thinking Foundation, and hosts a weekly radio show, Right Thinking with Steve Coplon that Donna is a regular guest on.

As Steve travels to prisons across the country with his financial literacy curriculum, Donna serves the community through local churches in food pantries and dedicates herself to family. She is ever present with her parents, helping them manage the daily struggle of living with Alzheimer's.

Steve has fought multiple myeloma cancer for eighteen years and prostate cancer for three. Donna is his constant companion, as they spend hours each day with the Lord, giving them strength to persevere.

Donna and Steve host a weekly Care Group (Bible study) in their home for the past eleven years. They are blessed with five children, seven beautiful grandchildren and another on the way. They live in Norfolk, VA and can be reached at www.RightThink.org.

CHAPTER III

Thankful For The Hard Times

By Deana Mitchell

In the fall of 2010, my husband and I had just moved from one Colorado mountain town to another, and I was figuring out my next step in life. It was the first time I left a job and did not have another one, but I was excited to enjoy hiking, skiing, and just being in nature for a while.

I had more time on my hands than ever in my adult life and was not sure how to handle that. Early 2011, I went through a third miscarriage and was having a hard time sleeping. I thought this third time would be different... no stressful job, not working long hours, I was resting, focusing on myself and doing my best to be healthy. At night, I would stay up on the couch grieving for the child I lost but also the loss of my career. It had been my identity for so many years; some would say it was a time of finding myself. I plunged head first into creating something to take my mind off the rest. Working with someone I found online to create a logo, she was in India and working when I should have been sleeping.

This went on for weeks, but I had no idea what direction this would take me in long term.

REALIZE WHAT YOU IMAGINE is the tagline I came up with when creating a name and logo... at the time, it was in the context of events and creating a vision for clients. Now after eight years, it ended up being more about what God wanted me to realize about myself, about HIM and about my husband.

John 15:5

[5] *"I am the vine; you are the branches. Whoever abides in me and I in him, he bears much fruit, for apart from me you can do nothing."*

Included in this chapter are abbreviated lyrics from three songs that I lived by over and over. It would not be a complete story about how God worked in my business and life without them. My hope is that they will also help you through something if you are reading this...

Confidence by Sanctus Real (lyrics shortened)

I'm not a warrior, I'm too afraid to lose
I feel unqualified for what

You're calling me to
But Lord with your strength,
I've got no excuse
'Cause broken people are
exactly who you use

So, give me faith like
Daniel in the lion's den
Give me hope like Moses in the wilderness
Give me a heart like David,
Lord be my defense
So, I can face my giants with confidence

You took a shepherd boy,
And made him a King
So, I'm gonna trust you
and give you everything
I'll be a conqueror, 'Cause you fight for me
I'll be a champion claiming your victory

When I started this journey I was lost, although I did not know it at the time. For decades, I always believed my job defined who I was and how I related to everyone in my life. I was so wrong... I realized the truth through this journey. I grew closer to Jesus through the hardships of starting and growing this business. Thankful for the hardest times, as those are when I grew the most and became the strongest.

Proverbs 3:6

⁶ *"Trust in the Lord with all your heart and lean not on your own understanding; in all your ways submit to him, and he will make your paths straight."*

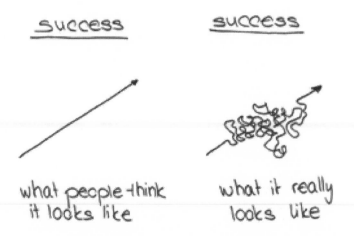

(image from officevibe.com)

The Orchestrator

Way before I ever thought of starting a business on my own, God had a plan. He perfectly choreographed my life to include many experiences that armed me with the knowledge and skills needed to be successful in my current situation. Move after move, job after job, I never saw the pattern or understood why any of it happened the way it did.

During my college years, I worked at the front desk of my dormitory at Colorado State, then at the LSU Faculty Club as the student banquet manager. For two summers I worked for Princess Cruises in Denali, Alaska. The first summer as a housekeeper and the second in the restaurant, mostly serving breakfast to the 5am wildlife tours into the park. Towards the end of my college career, I opened the Baton Rouge Copelands restaurant and became a headwaiter, then the lead bartender and a trainer.

After college I managed several restaurants:

- Lafitte's Landing in Donaldsonville, Louisiana (John Folse's restaurant that since burnt down)
- Borago in Grayton Beach, Florida (folded after hurricane Opal)
- Tib's in Destin, Florida (Charlie Goodson's venture outside of his famous restaurant in New Orleans)

- Macayo Restaurants in Phoenix, Arizona (Central, Tempe, Mesa and opening team for Ahwatukee)

During my time in Florida, I also built models and did some CAD work for an architect firm. At that point I did not really think about the future or what was next. I wanted to be good at my job and climb the corporate ladder but did not really have an end goal in mind.

The next chapter started with a position as Banquet Manager at the Landmark Hotel in Metairie, Louisiana, which was owned by Al Copeland. In addition to running banquets, I also was the acting F&B Director for part of that tenure.

Then came the opportunity that took me to Colorado... I was interviewing for the Banquet Manager position at the Silvertree Hotel (now the Westin) in Snowmass Village, Colorado. They asked if I would be interested in Conference Services and I was up for learning. So, I moved to the mountains! One summer I had a part time gig as a raft guide, which was one of my favorite jobs ever. I fell in love with the mountains, learned to ski and hiked Handies Peak, my first 14-er.

After a few years at the Silvertree, I was ready for a new challenge and moved to Georgia to work at a resort on Lake Lanier Islands. I could not imagine leaving Colorado and knew I would be back. Emerald Pointe Resort & Conference Center was an IACC property (International Association of Conference Centers) so it gave me an opportunity to learn a lot more about the meetings industry. Little did I know; this move was about meeting the love of my life. God had a plan, but I was a bit oblivious.

After getting married, I was itching to get back to Colorado. In 2005 we decided to make the move, and both worked at the Vail Cascade (now Hotel Talisa) in Vail, Colorado. We bought a house in Leadville and thought we were never leaving. We were heavily involved with the church there. I headed up an outreach with Angel Food Ministries that was such a blessing to our community. My husband was doing outreach at the hospital and local jail. I also worked as a part time ski instructor at Ski Cooper during those years. But then the 2008 recession came along and there was a different plan once again.

My husband was sent on several task force opportunities around the country and we were asked to move several times but declined. In 2009 he had an opportunity to move to Telluride, and since I had considered moving there before Georgia, I was excited. My current business was a result of this move, but my husband was sent on task force assignments again. Only this time it was for much longer periods of time and sometimes outside of the United States. The hardest was the year he spent seven months in Doha, Qatar training staff at a new property, working on achieving their five-diamond rating.

Ultimately, all the moves and jobs culminated in the perfect experience for what He had planned next for me and I became a small business owner out of necessity.

Deana Mitchell

Philippians 4:13

*13 "I can do all things through Christ
who strengthens me"*

The Facilitator

After being on my own for a few years, I got to the point of needing to employ help, but I never advertised. Each person who works for my company was put there in another way, which has resulted in the best team of rock stars! Below are just a few examples of how His plan unfolded.

During the early days, I worked for Telluride Ski & Golf and was helping open two new restaurants on the mountain. I was excited to use my F&B experience and met my first employee during that time. When I needed someone to help with events, she was willing and is still working part time for me years later.

Another person I met through a mutual co-worker has been a great friend, confidant and contract worker since the beginning. She is always there for me during hard times and good; her work with us is part-time but a benefit to us both; completely, a Godsend.

My first full-time employee reached out to me because she knew a client of mine. It happened in a year that my revenue grew almost three hundred percent and I was approaching people I knew about working with me full time, but none of them were ready for various reasons. This person is still on the team and has excelled at everything I throw at her!

Next was one of those people who were not ready prior but texted me out of the blue and asked if I was still looking for help. If I had not planted the seed a year or so prior; she would not have reached out. Of course, that was also at the perfect time and she is still on the team today.

In another huge growth year, a former employee at a hotel was looking for a new opportunity and I had been thinking about her and her experience for months. The previous company she worked for had sold, and she was not excited about the new role. I was ecstatic to get her on the team.

One of my early clients hired a photographer who I had never met. To this day he is our number one photographer for any type of event. Most of the pictures on our website were taken by him. He has been a great partner and always willing to help when we need images. Not to mention our clients LOVE his work!

I am blessed to have a team of amazing people who are hard workers, self-motivated and proactive. They act with integrity, kindness and respect for each other. God put each one of these people in my life, the right people at exactly the right time.

Isaiah 40:31

*31 "But those who hope in the Lord will
renew their strength. They will soar
on wings like eagles;
they will run and not grow weary,
they will walk and not be faint"*

The Protector

In the first few years, we had a small office space that worked perfectly in a great location. Then came an offer to move into a new space, which seemed great but turned out to be not such an opportunistic situation in the end. Lots of time and money were spent to get the space in good shape as it had been sitting empty for years. Improvements looked amazing and many friends and colleagues came out for our open house. It was perfect in many ways, but short-lived. The building sold and the new owners decided they did not want me there. I fought the decision and was devastated for a while, as we lost the time and money we put into the space. We moved back to the previous building in a bigger space that was not ideal. Things were difficult that year. Little did I know we would be moving again shortly and opening an office in Denver. Several people had asked me about moving to Denver because my business was growing, but I really wanted to stay in the mountains and had no intention of moving at the time.

I had been spending a lot of time all over the state and significant time in the city. Hotels were getting more and more expensive with all the growth, and I had to make a decision. I finally rented an apartment and committed to being there part-time. This is something I said for years I would not do; I loved being in the mountains too much and it meant more time apart from my husband. The tables had turned regarding who was never home, but still the same result… we were not in the same location full-time.

Once I made that decision to open the Denver office, my business sprouted! I believe that God was pushing me out of Telluride for a while and I was struggling to stay against His will. After making the move, everything changed for the better. God's timing is always perfect; we need to be content and patient.

Jesus said,

27 *"My sheep know my voice."*
John 10:27

After the move, the search was on for office space once again. I was looking at a space that was across the street from the new apartment, so I decided I would live there when in Denver. A few weeks later, my lawyer advised me not to sign the lease on that space. It was a state-owned building and a bit too risky for my small business.

Back to square one... I looked for weeks farther away from the place I rented but was not finding anything that worked. A friend made a comment to me about finding a place in an expensive part of town; it was close to my place and in a growing area. To make a long story short, I looked at about five places but only one had good exposure and I assumed I could not afford it. After a long day of meetings and seeing spaces, come to find out the perfect location was the most reasonably priced and we have been there for several years. The original comment to me was *"unless you are going to have an address on Broadway"* and we ended up at 1 Broadway!

God works in mysterious ways; it all worked out so perfectly. Our first full-time employee I told you about lives a few blocks away and walks to work every day with her dog.

Ephesians 3:20

20 "Now to Him who is able to do infinitely
more than all we ask or imagine,
according to His power
that is at work within us"

The Guardian

During my years as a small business owner, there has been no shortage of financial worries, from where the revenue will come from to paying taxes. With that being said, I have been truly blessed with abundance and perfect timing. Every year, except one, revenue has grown year over year. The best year was right under three hundred percent growth from the prior year. The early years were easier to manage with no employees and less revenue. As we grew and added to the team, payroll became our biggest expense, which is true for most small businesses.

I have found that prayer and trust is the best way for me to deal with financial worries. Be thankful for what is coming and ask Him to show you the way. It is in His hands; we are not in control. His plan was in the works way before we began thinking about it, and He has perfect timing. I have had days where I left the office wondering how I was going to pay something and the next morning the money is in my account, either from a new client or an unexpected payment.

Philippians 4:6

⁶ "Do not be anxious about anything,
but in everything, by prayer and petition,
with thanksgiving, present
your requests to God."

Sometimes you get new business from a client you met over a year ago. When you met them, they were friendly and you felt like you had a good connection, but they did not need you at the time. It is easy to walk away from those situations thinking that sales trip was not worth it, but God is always working behind the scenes to orchestrate His will in your life. Everything is amazingly orchestrated for His purpose even if we do not see the result for years.

Once I had someone contact me out of the blue because of a blog we posted, and it was about something unrelated but intrigued them. A phone call or an email can change everything, and you never know what the day will bring. The right people always seem to show up at the right time.

Two years in a row, we won an award that we did not even know we were up for! U.S. Partner of the Year in 2017 & 2018 from Global DMC Partners, completely unexpected. That brought unexpected press and exposure. It gave us credibility to customers who had never heard of us. I have also written articles for industry magazines and blogs that get exposure without spending on advertising.

That does not mean any of it has been easy. God pushes me every day to be better, mostly to lean on Him more for understanding. The most valuable lesson I have learned is about being content, which is not an easy thing. Being happy, patient and compassionate during hard times takes strength and faith.

Psalm 105:4

[4] *"Look to the Lord and his strength;*
seek his face always."

Joshua 1:9

[9] *"Have I not commanded you? Be strong and*
courageous. Do not be terrified; do not be
discouraged, for the LORD your God will be
with you wherever you go."

When I was growing up, there was a small-framed picture in the bathroom that said, *"Bloom where you are planted."* It did not mean that much to me when I was a kid, but that is exactly what contentment is all about. Being content has been the biggest lesson for me, one that changed everything and helped me cope with anxiety. Understanding that God has me in this place for a reason is crucial to my outlook on life. I need to do my best with whatever comes my way, to show my faith in Him and to be an example for others. Fulfilling what He needs me to do so He can use my story later for His good. So, giving thanks to God for this day, this place you are in, and for His will in your life is my mantra. I thank God every day for what is coming. I do this because I know His plans are better that I can imagine.

In my home, I have some sayings that are daily reminders, here are a few:

- Life isn't about waiting for the storm to pass, it's about learning to dance in the rain
- The task ahead of us is never as great as the Power behind us
- The will of God never takes you to where the Grace of God will not protect you
- Peace starts with a smile
- God doesn't call the qualified, He qualifies the called
- I am in this place because God wants me here (Bloom where you are planted)
- If you can stay positive in a negative situation, you win

- Everything comes to you at the right time, be patient and trust in the process

Daily I search out sermons or readings to help me understand situations and what God says about what I might be going through. Recently I have read about a couple of things that intrigued me, things that put some perspective into my thoughts.

1. *God wants us to spread His word and His light*, although we are given these things without earning them. Imagine there was a rich man who would write you a check for one million dollars and tell you that you must give it all away as fast as you can... then he will give you more and you continue the process. You cannot keep the money. This is just like God's love, you cannot earn it, it is endless, and he wants you to give it away as fast as you can!

"When I love God most,
I will love others best".

2. In the book 7 Habits of Highly Successful People, there is an exercise that talks about your funeral.

There will be four speakers, what do you hope they say? What is YOUR definition of success and how would you like to be remembered? Come up with seven words...

Below are my seven words that I hope describe me when I am gone from this earth. This exercise helped me make a list of my priorities and how I should conduct myself to show these qualities first. How do you hope to be remembered?

A. Integrity
B. Kindness
C. Honesty
D. Faithful
E. Content
F. Helped Others
G. Love

Lamentations 3:25-26

[25] *"The Lord is good to those whose hope is in Him, to the one who seeks Him;*
[26] *it is good to wait quietly for the salvation of the Lord"*

My conclusion in all of this is to be thankful for the challenges and rough times. Although that is not our instinct, it is what God instructs us to do. The hardest times usually precede the greatest successes.

The lyrics below have been instrumental in this for me…

Do It Again by Elevation Worship (lyrics shortened)

Walking around these walls,
I thought by now they'd fall
But You have never failed me yet
Waiting for change to come,
Knowing the battle's won
For You have never failed me yet

Your promise still stands
Great is Your faithfulness, faithfulness
I'm still in Your hands
This is my confidence,
you've never failed me yet

I know the night won't last,
Your Word will come to pass
My heart will sing Your praise again
Jesus, you're still enough,
Keep me within Your love
My heart will sing Your praise again

I've seen You move,
You move the mountains
And I believe, I'll see You do it again
You made a way, where there was no way
And I believe, I'll see You do it again

You've never failed me yet
And I never will forget

When this crazy business journey started, I had no clue what I was getting into; I just needed to make money for my family. God has taught me so much through these years and most of all I have learned of His love for me, it is endless and reckless and beautiful.

I would not be telling the whole story if I did not say how loving, giving and supportive my husband has been through all of this. We have been apart for the better part of the last nine years; the hardest of those times were when he was in the Middle East for so many months.

Our marriage is stronger than ever and Michael is the reason my faith is so strong today. Because of his influence, I strive to be a better Christian and a better person in general. His mantra is God, family, job and it is obvious to all who know him. I am so blessed to call him my husband. Our marriage was absolutely God's plan, but that story is for another time.

Leadville, Mt Elbert (2006) Georgia (2004) Telluride (2012)

At many stages in my life, I have run from my faith and thought I knew better. If I just attain this or that, I can make it on my own and accomplish my hopes. That thought process has gotten me in trouble… it is all about joy and peace, which is found in You and You alone. Lord, I pray that you help us quit running and just abide in You. Help us to be faithful as You have been faithful time and time again. You will always remain in pursuit of us, so let us quit trying to live on our own. You are where our help and purpose come from, where our peace and joy are found.

Psalm 46:10

[10] *"Be still and know that I am God"*

"Life doesn't get to define you.
Your highs and lows don't get to define
you because the God of this universe
already did. Yes, you still have the
disappointments,
but we can bounce back.
Don't be defined by the world and
how people see you.
I do not know what the future holds,
but I know who holds my future.
In that there is peace,
in that there is satisfaction. "

— Tim Tebow

I believe that I am on this earth to spread the light of Jesus and His promise of hope. I have learned that the best way for me to do that is for God to use me through the hard times I have endured. He continually uses my past situations to help me, and others who show up in my life.

So, I am thankful for the scars…

Scars by I am They (lyrics shortened)

Waking up to a new sunrise,
Looking back from the other side
I can see now with open eyes,
Darkest water and deepest pain
I wouldn't trade it for anything,
cause my brokenness brought me to You
And these wounds are a story You'll use

So, I'm thankful for the scars, 'Cause
without them I wouldn't know Your heart
And I know they'll always tell of who You are,
so forever I am thankful for the scars
Now I'm standing in confidence,
With the strength of Your faithfulness
And I'm not who I was before,
No, I don't have to fear anymore
I can see, I can see, How You delivered me
In Your hands, In Your feet,

Deana Mitchell

I found my victory
I'm thankful for Your scars, 'Cause without
them I wouldn't know Your heart
And with my life I'll tell of who You are,
so forever I am thankful

Deana Mitchell, CMP DMCP CCSE | Bio

Deana strives every day to shine the light of Jesus through compassion and kindness.

She grew up in the Methodist church but spent years away from her faith in her younger adult life. After rediscovering her faith and meeting Michael, they spent nine months prior to their wedding in a couples bible study group. Deana sites that as being the foundation of their strong marriage from the beginning.

Deana Mitchell is the Owner & Founder of Realize Colorado, a Global DMC Partner. Realize is an award-winning destination management company that serves the great state of Colorado. Her background includes almost three decades in the hospitality industry and a Bachelor of Architecture from Louisiana State University. In 2005, she earned the Certified Meeting Professional designation, in 2012 the Destination Management Certified Professional designation and in 2015 the Customer Certified Sales Expert designation.

https://www.linkedin.com/in/deanamitchell/

www.realizecolorado.com

CHAPTER IV

Discover Your Gift
By Taft Mohair II

*"A person's purpose in life is always
connected to their giftedness."*

—John C. Maxwell

The purpose of this book is to provide you with insights and tools for discovering and developing your gift! When we do this effectively it puts us in the middle of our purpose! Living in purpose glorifies God and brings us joy and fulfillment!

What Are You Running To?

In 2011, my friend Renesha said to me *"I am tired of asking for permission to live my life!"*. Her statement arrested my attention! I had experienced this same frustration and I immediately identified with her anguish. I knew I had a plan that would benefit her.

Renesha is what most of us would consider as successful. She has earned a bachelor's and a master's degree in accounting and she's employed with a very successful company in Houston Texas. The truth of the matter is millions of people have earned degrees and certifications in disciplines that they are good at and even great at, but it is not the area that brings them the greatest joy and fulfillment.

Around 1995-1997, I was in the same situation, but I had never articulated the pain the way she had. I thought about her statement for days! The career frustration memories began to flood my thoughts. One memory in particular was very lucid. I recalled how I had concluded that I was clear about what I was running FROM (*Pain!*). But I was not clear about what I was running TO (*Purpose!*).

God Will Never Leave Us!

As I went through this career frustration, I began to look for a way out of corporate America. I started my first network marketing business in 1996, as a WAY OUT of corporate America!! I wisely prayed about walking away from my job as an engineer. Without a response from God, I foolishly made my decision and walked away. I did not want to be in corporate America as an engineer, but I had no clue what I really wanted to do. Not only that, I did not know how to pray about career, purpose, gifting, or passion.

What makes it worst, I did not know, that I did not know how to pray about purpose and gifting! I was oblivious to the fact that it was not time for me to walk away! I had not learned enough, and I had not earned enough to be a full-time entrepreneur.

After walking away, I began to struggle financially. I destroyed my excellent credit rating. I depleted my bank accounts. I damaged friendships. But God was constant! It seemed like this period of my life was a financial valley, but God never left me. Even in that valley God kept demonstrating His love.

Since my bills were screaming *"GET A JOB"*, I began to interview for engineering positions and no doors opened. At this time, I did not know my purpose in life, but I knew that I really enjoyed sharing insights with people that would empower them to do better in life. So, my next step was obvious, become a teacher.

I visited my high school Booker T. Washington/High School for the Engineering Professions (BTW/HSEP) and shared with them my desire to work as a substitute teacher. They hired me immediately. I served at BTW/HSEP as a dedicated substitute teacher for that entire school year in various roles English, Spanish, Chemistry, and more! The BTW/HSEP experience launched me into my next teaching position as an Algebra teacher at Sterling High School. The experience at Sterling pushed me to my next position at Project Chrysalis Middle School as the math teacher for sixth, seventh, and eighth grade.

My experience during those 6 years in education helped to reveal my purpose in life. I took the success, leadership, and business principles that I was introduced to in network marketing and I became a committed student. I read books, attended trainings, and listened to audio programs by Napoleon Hill, John Maxwell, Les Brown, Tony Evans, Jim Rohn, Bishop T.D. Jakes, Dr. Bill Winston, and Brian Tracy; just to name a few. I took those principles and began to simplify them and teach them to my students! The results were life changing. Increased self-esteem and as a result their grades increased. That platform allowed me to impact students, the families, and even some of my colleagues.

Please understand that everything was NOT perfect! Discovering and developing my gifts and figuring out my life's purpose was a PROCESS! A very challenging process! But I began to understand that teaching people how to transform their lives gave me tremendous joy and gave them solutions that formal education never taught. More importantly, it gave God tremendous glory!

I want to share with you three questions that you can address and start your process of gift discovery.

How do I discover my gifts?

Millions of people get up every day and pour their life into a job that provides no joy. School does not teach how to discover your gifts!

What are you passionate about?

The purpose that God has shaped us for is connected to the things that we are most passionate about. We may not know our purpose in life as children or even as adults. But early in our lives we develop an understanding or a drawing to those things that we are passionate about or that we love. Think about the experiences that give you the most joy. That is a clue! Unfortunately, we are not taught this growing up and we often do not give it the attention that it deserves. I encourage you to consider this question overtime and put your answers on paper.

How do others view your talents and gifts?

As mentioned earlier typically there is no teaching on discovering your purpose or identifying your gifting, so we tend not to notice the things that we are passionate about or the gifts, talents, and abilities that often set us apart from everyone else. So, one approach that many people can leverage is asking people who are close to them, *"What do you think my gifts, talents, and abilities are?"* I encourage you to ask people that you trust and put these answers on paper and give it careful consideration through prayer.

Ask God!

God is the source of the gift. He has shaped us with a specific purpose for our life and given us gifts that empower us to accomplish that purpose. So, the best source of information in regard to our gifting and our purpose in life is to go to the One who gave us the gift and the purpose. My encouragement for you is to invest a season of prayer around your gifts, talents, abilities, purpose and mission. Not only will you receive answers to your question but your relationship with God is going to increase. Your reliance on God is going to increase. As God unfolds the purpose and gifting that He has allowed you to be a steward of you are going to grow in the love of God. As you begin to deliver this gifting to the world and live in your purpose you are going to give God glory in a very natural way on a daily basis.

4 Tools for The Process!

There are several ways to approach these three questions. We will share four effective strategies that you can employ starting today as you seek answers to these three questions.

Journal

As mentioned earlier as you are gaining answers and developing clarity around these three questions, do all of it on paper. Many people simply call this journaling. Writing the questions, answers, and your thoughts on both will add amazing clarity to your process.

A Season of Prayer

It is very important not only to pray about these three questions, but you want to dedicate a season of prayer to the questions. Prayer is the believer's weapon for establishing God's will on earth as it is in Heaven. It is God's will that you walk in purpose. A season of prayer looks like a 30, 60, or 90-day commitment. It some instances it might be longer. If you have a disciplined prayer life now this will most likely be as simple as a *making a decision*.

Those of us who are building a disciplined prayer life, here are a few suggestions:

1. Pick your timeframe, 30, 60, or 90 days!
2. Decide on 3, 5, or 7 days a week!
3. Pick a time of the day!
4. Put it on your physical calendar and or smart phone (set reminders)!
5. Talk to your Father from your heart!

Wise Counsel

Proverbs tell us that *a lack of counsel leads to failure, but many advisers lead us to success.* Allowing people to provide wise counsel to you as you navigate these waters can make a huge difference. People in different circles will use the word counselor, some use advisor, some use mentor! The key is having someone who cares about your growth and success that is further along in the success process to provide wisdom and insight that will guide you in your process.

Assessment Tools

The final tool is in the area of assessments. There are spiritual gifts assessments on the Internet that you can access at no cost and some that cost, such as Team Ministry: Gifted to Serve and or Lifeway. In addition to spiritual gift assessments you can also take advantage of personality and behavioral assessments like Birkman, DISC, and Strength Finders. After completing a profile, if you agree or disagree, be open and receptive to the insights. Add these insights to your journal and prayer time. God will begin to reveal to you a greater understanding of your gifts, talents, and abilities.

3 Strategies for Developing Your Gift

Anything that is not growing is dying. In the case of your gifting it is important to understand that if we don't develop the gift it will never grow. If the gift never grows you will never be able to utilize the gift at its optimum. Combining these strategies with your daily schedule positions you to be intentional about your growth process.

Serve

Mahatma Gandhi stated, *"the best way to find yourself is to lose yourself in the service of others."* Identify for profit and nonprofit organizations that will allow you to serve in the area of your gifting. As you are developing your gift think of this service as practice. Usain Bolt had to practice becoming a gold medal Olympian in track. He had to practice 6 or 7 days a week, 7 to 10 hours a day developing his *'running gift'*. If you want to become a gold medal Olympian in the area of your gifting, I encourage you to serve. Focus on giving versus getting! Focus on how many seeds you can sow in the lives of men, women, and children. The more seeds that you sow the greater the harvest you are going to reap and greater your ability to deliver your gift. Keep in mind, you may not reap where you sowed but it is a guarantee that you will reap.

Constant and Never-Ending Improvement

Committing yourself to constant and never-ending improvement, also called CANI, will position you to be one of the best at what you do. Everyone embraces the idea of improvement but words like commit & constant tend to trip us up! Let's look at the simplicity of CANI! The average annual return of the S&P 500 is 10%. An S&P 500 return of 12%, 20% or even 50% means you are beating the market and earning above average returns. Imagine if you improved at 12% per year, every year! Most people NEVER commit to a plan and become intentional about growth. 12% improvement per year, every year, is only 1% improvement per month. So, the question becomes, *"Can I improve by 1% every 30 days?"* Of course! The key is getting a plan and committing. Imagine doing this for the next year and improving by 12%, building new habits, increasing your productivity, strengthening your gifting and adding value to society in a manner that gives you great fulfillment. Guess what, IT DOESN'T STOP!!! The following year you duplicate the plan and process but because you are better, you grow at 2% per month and 24% for the year! I am intentionally using moderate numbers. I have seen people grow at 30% and 40% in one year. Conversely, I have seen MOST people not grow at all. No improvement spiritually, financially, relationally and specifically no growth in their area of passion and or gifting. Not because they could not, they simply DID NOT, commit to a plan! If we expect our children to grow, much less our investments, we should grow also.

Identify A Mentor

"When I was a young lawyer, there were other women and men in the firm who took me under their wing. Sometimes mentors don't find you – sometimes you seek them out. You shouldn't hesitate to plop herself in someone's office and ask them to be that support.... Oftentimes, they're flattered and glad to lend a hand. So, I would encourage any reader to seek out a mentor, then follow through and be very focused and persistent."

— Michelle Obama

One of the most successful strategies that you can employ is identifying a mentor.

Having a mentor who is actively providing wise counsel will not only show you what you should do but it will also show you what not to do. The two previous strategies build on the mentor strategy. If a person is going to take time to be a mentor one of the first areas of concern that they will evaluate is what are you already doing. In addition, when you serve and do the steps required to improve, you automatically put yourself in a position to meet people who are further along in the success process. These same individuals may be willing to mentor you.

Mentors initially may come in the form of books, seminars, podcast, and audio programs. Integrating a person's wisdom that you collect through print media and electronic media into your growth plan will pay tremendous dividends. I know for a fact that my ability and desire to learn from these different mediums not only assisted me in developing my gift and clarifying my purpose in life, but it also made me stand out from my colleagues. This communicated to people who were willing to take time to mentor me that I was a project worth investing in!

Conclusion

Discovering and developing your gifting brings massive joy to your life. Walking in your gift brings tremendous joy to the lives of those you serve. In the tenth chapter of the Gospel according to John we get a glimpse at the enemy's objective and the objective of our Lord and Savior, Jesus the Christ! *The enemy's objective is to steal, kill, and destroy.* When we fail to discover and develop our gifting, we are indirectly assisting the enemy in his objective. The objective of Jesus coming is that *we may have life and have it more abundantly.* When we do the work to discover and develop our gifting, we are assisting our Lord and Savior in accomplishing His objective. Simply put walking in our gifting brings abundance to someone's life! I encourage you, do the work and go & do great exploits and glorify God!

Taft Mohair II | Bio

Taft is a passionate, dynamic, and entertaining speaker with an excellent ability to inspire, inform and empower people with simple, yet profound insights that move them toward success in all walks of life.

Taft addresses thousands of men, women and children each year on the subjects of personal, professional and spiritual development. His energized talks and seminars on success, leadership, self-esteem, teamwork, spiritual growth, and goal achievement bring about immediate change and long-term results.

Taft is president of Empowered Insights, a training and development company based, in Houston, Texas. He is a certified leader with the John Maxwell Team in the area of Speaking, Training, and Coaching.

Prior to founding his company, Taft was successful as an engineer, educator and entrepreneur. As an International Motivational Speaker, he has given memorable keynotes to students, faculty and staff, small business owners and corporate executives.

Taft Mohair

info@taftmohair.com / www.TaftMohair.com

CHAPTER V

The Journey is Love
By Geoff Hudson-Searle

*'Our lives are measured in choices we have
made along the path we call living, each
compass point, a possibility, each step, an
opportunity, seemingly random, each decision
moves us inexorably in a direction both
unknown and yet somehow familiar for upon
reflection, the strength we find in choosing, or
the surrender of letting all unfold leads us to the
place we started from when we made that
first choice to be here again*

— Richard Cohn

What is Love

What is love in our now world? The Oxford dictionary has its definition as:

'Love' /lʌv/

A feeling or disposition of deep affection or fondness for someone, typically arising from a recognition of attractive qualities, from natural affinity, or from sympathy and manifesting itself in concern for the other's welfare and pleasure in his or her presence (distinguished from sexual love at sense 4a); great liking, strong emotional attachment; (similarly) a feeling or disposition of benevolent attachment experienced towards a group or category of people, and (by extension) towards one's country or another impersonal object of affection. With of, for, to, towards.

'In 1611 within The Sacred Bible (King James) Daniel. 1:9

[9] *'God had brought Daniel into*
favour and tender love
with the Prince of the Eunuches.'

A large amount of discussion in entrepreneur and business groups has been around the subject of love and passion in the workplace for what we do. Whilst I understand this is a very subjective matter, exactly what is love and how do we apply passion to our thinking and execute this in our daily work and everyday lives?

There simply is not a one-size-fits-all formula for discovering what you're passionate about and then transitioning to a new or existing career. That being said, I have learned a few things about doing what you love for work—and this was the précis for my first book *Freedom After the Sharks*, my second book *Meaningful Conversations* and recent book collaborations.

Some big questions in life centre around love. Why people should live in love and why we are not communicating and forging meaningful and unconditional relationships, love is simple right...?

Love is simple when we understand the true meaning of unconditional love. The kind of love that transforms and transcends us as human beings to a higher level of consciousness, in those moments when we truly love, we become alive, we feel passion, we feel life in every breath. Love is life, at the core of everything we do on this life path it is love that is the driving force.

I believe we are not forming unconditional relationships because of the environment we live in, the world of technology, the fast paced, instant access, immediate response world, we receive things immediately, therefore we expect everything instantly, we are conditioned to having it all "*now*".

As with the greatest things in life, the magic only happens when things are given time to breathe, when thoughts are clear, when the mind is at peace. It is only in this environment that unconditional love can flourish. The magic ingredient to unconditional love is finding peace within your own mind; for when your mind is at peace others will be at peace. It is with this level of peace that bliss exists.

Listen to what your relationships are telling you: love and listening go hand in hand. To love unconditionally you must have the ability to listen to what another person is asking of you; not listening to what your emotions and desires are telling you, but really listening to what that person is asking of you. When we listen to what another requires above our own needs then we create trust, and we create understanding; when we understand things, the fear goes away. It is only then can we become selfless, allowing the time for love to flourish unconditionally.

Family and partner love

Having grown with my grandmother and grandfather, watching their beautiful relationship of 50 years and unconditional love. Still, the question remains in the new era of a fast-paced technological world and life, can love last forever?

Elements of my grandparent's beautiful marriage can, and should, be a real living example of a lasting, loving relationship. There's no reason that "*love forever*" cannot exist, and in fact, relationships with so much love and sustainability should exist with the partner you call your love or spouse. True love is a decision of the will. It's a choice based on many factors, including that "*in love*" feeling you have for your love or spouse. Such a feeling can be built upon with tenderness, romantic gestures, and caring choices all along the way.

Can love last forever? Yes, indeed it can. Real love is made up of more than just that wonderful feeling that makes your heart go and butterflies in the stomach when you first meet. We might call that stage of love infatuation.

True love doesn't begin until two people really get to know each other and from there build a stronger connection, loving rapport, and a lasting commitment. Such a relationship takes work, understanding, compromises, flexibility, forgiveness, good communication and much more. Chemistry is a part of it as well, but even beyond chemistry and the physical attraction, a love that will last forever is based on a strong decision and will to stay together.

Staying together is a lifetime commitment, but just staying together is not good enough. For true love to last forever, it requires two people to remain open, honest, and to change and grow not just individually, but also as a couple. As changes take place, a successful couple manages to flow with the changes, and love each other through them all. So, can love last forever? Truly, there's no reason for love to ever end!

Scientists have discovered true love. Brain scans have proved that a small number of couples can respond with as much passion after 20 years as most people exhibit only in the first flush of love.

The findings overturn the conventional view that love and sexual desire peak at the start of a relationship and then decline as the years pass.

A team from Stony Brook University in New York scanned the brains of couples that had been together for 20 years and compared them with those of new lovers. They found that about one in 10 of the mature couples exhibited the same chemical reactions when shown photographs of their loved ones as people commonly do in the early stages of a relationship.

Previous research suggested that the first stages of romantic love, a rollercoaster ride of mood swings and obsessions that psychologists call limerence, start to fade within 15 months. After 10 years the chemical tide has ebbed away.

The scans of some of the long-term couples, however, revealed that elements of limerence mature, enabling them to enjoy what a new report calls *"intensive companionship and sexual liveliness."*

The reactions of these long-term couples to pictures of their beloved were identified on MRI brain scans as a burst of pleasure-producing dopamine more commonly seen in couples who are gripped in the first flush of lust.

"The findings go against the traditional view of romance – that it drops off sharply in the first decade – but we are sure it's real," said Arthur Aron, a psychologist at Stony Brook.

So can couples and relationships stay together for a lifetime of love, happiness and togetherness? Absolutely, the question is how much do you want to have a lifetime partner.

Passion from the heart

History has proven that some of the most passionate, successful people are those who have sacrificed many of their needs to push toward one all-encompassing goal.

We all have different advantages, some based on good fortune and some based on choices we have previously made. We can only ever start from where we are. If we have the strength to play our hands, instead of questioning why we don't hold different cards, then we can decide at any time to work toward doing what we love.

The important thing is to remember that so much is still possible. We all deserve to enjoy the way we spend our days. If we're willing to dream, work hard, learn, and navigate uncertainty, we all have the potential to do it

I was sharing coffee with one of my great author friends recently, discussing one of my books *"Meaningful Conversations"* and we discussed how do we write life's tapestry if the heart is blocked.

The feeling I am describing is when you sit down to write and instead of feeling an energetic creative flow, you sit completely paralyzed, staring at your computer screen & seething at the injustice of your lack of creative life, many people describe this as writer's block.

Studies have found writer's block to be a simpler problem: an inability to allow the creative process to flow because of unhappiness, this happened to me personally when I wrote *"Freedom after the Sharks"*. But there are different kinds of unhappiness, and it's the writers job to be honest about which one they're suffering from and in some respect this can be a very important part of a writer revealing the truth about his or her unhappiness, the truth is always revealed in writing as in photography Robert Louis Stevenson, wrote: *"I doubt if these islanders are acquainted with any other mode of representation but photography; so that the picture of an event (on the old melodrama principle that 'the camera cannot lie, would appear strong proof of its occurrence."*

Woody Allen makes fun of writer's block. He wrote a play called *"Writer's Block"*, and he wrote, directed, and starred in a film called *"Deconstructing Harry"*, in which the protagonist, Harry Block, tells his therapist; *'For the first time in my life I experience writers block....Now this, to me, is unheard of....I start these short stories and I can't finish them....I can't get into my novel at all.....because I took an advance.'*

Writers block immediately disqualifies Harry Block from being Woody Allen because Woody Allen is one of the most productive filmmakers of his and possibly any generation. Between 1965 and 2014, Allen was credited in for than sixty-six films as a director, writer or actor, often and more than not, all three. To take writing alone; Allen has written forty-nine full-length theatrical films, eight stage plays, two television films and two short films, in less than sixty six years, a rate of a script a year.

I have studied Woody Allen and when you look at his miraculous life you can ascertain that time was of the most importance to his every moment, this quote really says everything about his passion for writing:

'I never like to let any time go unused. When I walk somewhere in the morning, I still plan what I'm going to think about, which problem I'm going to tackle. I may say, this morning I'm

going to think of titles. When I get in the shower in the morning, I try to use that time. So much of my time is spent thinking because that's the only way to attack these writing problems'

Allen had many philosophies, which I admire but I feel the one that resonates with me the most is intrinsic motivation, '*self-motivation is the only motivation*'. In life there are natural forces that we cannot guide or control, but I have learned as a writer that the power to create always comes from within, you will see some of my personal quotes where I use '*never, never give up on your dreams*', the truth always comes down to how much you really want to achieve your dream, do you like the idea, or are your driven to achieve your idea.

One of my mentors many years ago would say to me stop procrastinating and just do what needs to be achieved, I have never forgotten these words.

Writing is subjective, each and every one of us has a distinctive view, like and dislike to genre, fiction, non-fiction, biographical or fantasy, you will never please everyone, but with passion you can create your best.

Much of writer's block comes from fear of the unknown, worry across what others will think, Woody Allen also quoted why indifference is so important, something that we all can relate to in business today, when he said: '*longevity is an achievement, yes, but the achievement that I'm going for is to try to make great films. That has eluded me over the decades.'*

I would like to point out some thoughts on passion, I believe every single person on the planet has passion whether we like to recognise this or not, passion if directed in the right way or focus can create amazing things, however passion in the opposite can destroy. So many of us, for reasons only we can answer, do not implement, execute or action our true and resolute passion/s. Unfulfilled passion creates a cavity between our present and our true potential. You have all heard of the saying *'if only'* or *'it might have been different if'*, we all need to chase our dreams, you need to be careful what you wish for, because it may just come true. Unfulfilled passion can only create negative and malicious intent, which takes us away from our ultimate desires and purpose in life.

Steve Brunkhorst once said:

'As we weave the tapestries of our lives, we gradually begin to see our designs from a wider angle of years. We may or may not be pleased with what we see. Yet, no design—not in the living world—is carved in stone. We have the gift of free will to change our designs as we wish. We are each a thread in the tapestry of our human family. Our outcome is woven of endless

possibilities, because we can choose from a
universe of endless possibilities. Every person
can make a difference. Each thread is a
possibility, chosen by the design of divine
imagination. Our lifetime designs arise from
our divine gifts, unique talents, desires,
thoughts, choices, and actions. At times, old
choices—old threads—wear out. We see the past
while we live in the present, and we can replace
the old…with new ideas, new choices, and new
actions. We can view the future through today's
eyes, and time blends all experiences, dark and
light, into an awareness of authentic joy. May
you live joyfully and abundantly today and
throughout every season of life!'

Some points on Love and Passion

1. Do what you love and the money will follow.

If there's one thing that holds us back from pursuing our passions, it's the fear of not being able to take care of ourselves. It's what keeps us in unfulfilling jobs: the guaranteed salary that's enough.

But this ignores the fact that succeeding in anything requires a great deal of work and uncertainty. Risk is always part of the equation. For everyone who has made a good living doing something they enjoy, there is countless other equally talented people who were not able to do it.

This does not mean we should not pursue our passions; it just means we're more apt to feel satisfied doing it if we define success in terms beyond financial gain. That might mean we need to live on less. It might mean we need to balance our passion with other work.

Do what you love and enjoyment will follow. Do what you love and you will feel more fulfilled. Do what you love and the money will seem less relevant. These things I have found are true.

2. Leap and the net will appear.

Fear can be too much to make a leap, especially when you have no idea where you'll land or how. A lot of us get caught in the planning stage because we want to know with absolute certainty we won't make a mistake we'll one day regret.

So, we wait, we gather information, we imagine all possible outcomes and plan to avoid negative ones, and generally anchor ourselves with good intentions that, sometimes, never lead to action.

Confidence is that we need to have faith that we won't fall flat on our faces. But the reality is that we sometimes we will.

What's important to realise is that we are strong enough to get back up if this happens, and we can do it knowing that every fall is valuable. Every time a net does not appear, we learn a little more about how to weave one for ourselves. We also learn to be comfortable in the drop, which, if we're honest, is where we always live. Life is uncertain, whether we take large risks or not.

It's not just the leaps that dictate our success; it's our capacity for soaring through the unknown, and our willingness to learn from the landing.

3. Do what you love, and you'll never work a day in your life.

With any job or business, you often need to do things you would not choose to do.

But that's not the only reason doing what you love can feel like work. There's also the inevitability that most tasks feel different when they become things we need to do to earn. When the monetary compensation increases, suddenly the money becomes the motivation, and as a result, it feels less enjoyable.

I suspect this comes down to freedom: we tend to best enjoy the things we feel we're doing entirely by choice. Since work, in any form, requires commitment that supersedes our moment-to-moment whims, we need to know going in that even the most enjoyable paths will have their ups and downs.

The Journey of Love is God

It is said that *He who is filled with the gift of Piety finds the practice of his religion, not a burdensome duty, but a delightful service.*

'Where there is love, there is no labor'.

As Christians we have been very good at bringing the Gospel message for people to receive Jesus into a person's heart. But we have neglected an important part of the Gospel and that is about living in God's heart. God's desire is that we would become united with Him. We are to dwell in Him and He in us. *...truly our fellowship is with the Father and with His Son Jesus Christ.* (1 John 1:3) Fellowship is the Greek word *koinonia*, which literally means partnership and communion. God desires that our heart becomes one with His heart.

He desires to fill our heart and our entire being. He desires to have His hands in our hands and His feet in our feet so that we will go and do what He desires.

Jesus says,

⁵ "I am the vine, you are the branches. He who abides (lives and remains) in Me, and I in him, bears much fruit; for without Me you can do nothing"
John 15:5

Only what we do in Christ has eternal value.

Living in Christ is where you are transformed into a new person.

2 Corinthians 5:17

¹⁷ Therefore, if anyone is in Christ, he is a new creation; old things have passed away; behold, all things have become new.

The revelation of being in Christ changes our concept of who we are. It is in Christ where His personality is united with our personality and we take on a new personality. We become a new person with a new attitude, new behaviors, new likes, and dislikes.

We do not really know who we are until we see ourselves in Christ, because our life is hidden in Him.

Colossians 3:2-3

2 Set your mind on things above,
not on things on the earth.
3 For you died, and your life is
hidden with Christ in God.

It is a good to take an honest look deep inside your own heart to see what changes need to be made for the sake of your relationship with God. We all must depend upon God to make the changes in our hearts that are necessary for us to be more like Him. We even need God to help us in evaluating our own hearts in the light of His word and by His Holy Spirit.

Jeremiah 17:9-10

9 The heart is deceitful above all things and
beyond cure. Who can understand it?
10 "I the LORD search the heart and examine
the mind, to reward a man according to his
conduct, according to what his deeds deserve."

Jesus taught that we are defiled by what comes out of our hearts.

Mark 7:20-23

20 And He said, "What comes out of a man, that defiles a man.
21 For from within, out of the heart of men, proceed evil thoughts, adulteries, fornications, murders,
22 thefts, covetousness, wickedness, deceit, lewdness, an evil eye, blasphemy, pride, foolishness.
23 "All these evil things come from within and defile a man."

What we think about is what is in our heart, and is what we become.

Romans 12:2

² And do not be conformed to this world, but be transformed by the renewing of your mind, that you may prove what is that good and acceptable and perfect will of God.

The word transformed is the Greek word *metamorphoo* it is where we get the word metamorphosis from, the word used to describe the transformation of a caterpillar into a butterfly.

Final thought

My final thought in the matter is that a society cannot flourish without some sense of shared purpose and belief system and most importantly love. Even in adversity, God directs us to glorify Him in every circumstance of life. Guided by its light, we put first things first, and prize the friendship of God beyond all else. *'Knowledge is a fountain of life to him that possesses it'*. The current pursuit of self-realisation will not work. If your sole duty is to achieve the best for yourself, life becomes just too stressful and too lonely, and you will be set up to fail. Instead, you need to feel you exist for something larger, and that very thought will take you to sharing this vision in support of others. *'find something more important than you are,'* philosopher Dan Dennett once said in discussing the secret of happiness, *'and dedicate your life to it.'* But how, exactly, do we find that? Surely, it isn't by luck. I myself am a firm believer in the power of curiosity and choice as the engine of fulfillment, but precisely how you arrive at your true calling is an intricate and highly individual dance of discovery. Still, there are certain factors and certain choices on your journey to love that make it easier and more worthwhile...Everyone has a story, despite difficulties in family life and professional setbacks, the journey to love is the learning's we all have, we all possess the determination, drive and skills to create a foundation and happy life, the bigger question is if we choose to use these skills.....for the great of good.

Geoffrey Hudson-Searle | Bio

Geoff is an international commercial director, Digital Non-Executive Director, CMO, CEO, CCO, thought leader, mentor and strategist, lecturing regularly on the principles of integrated strategy at worldwide forums and events, rated by Agilience as a Top 250 Harvard Business School authority, covering strategic management and management consulting, and has over 25 years of experience in the business and management arena, an author of his first book 'Freedom after the Sharks' his second book 'Meaningful Conversations' and more recently he was asked to write a chapter being one of 11 thought leaders contributing to 'Journeys to Success Volume 9'. A member and fellow of the Institute of Directors, associate of The Business Institute of Management, a co-founder and board member of the Neustar International Security Council (NISC) and a distinguished member of the Advisory Council for The Global Cyber Academy. He holds a Masters degree in Business Administration. Having worked for corporate companies Citibank N.A, MICE Group Plc, Enigma Design, MMT Inc, Kaspersky Laboratory, Bartercard Plc, and RG Group around the world, Geoff has vast international experience working with SME and International clients. International clients with whom Geoff has worked include the British Government, HP, Compaq, BT, Powergen, Intel, ARM, Watsila Group, Atari, Barclays Bank, Societe Generale, Western Union, Chase and Volvo. Geoff has worked in a broad range of industries including software, technology and banking which has given him a range of different experiences and perspectives of what can work, the importance of good people, process and how these can be applied and amplified to deliver results in different scenarios and paradigms. Geoff is known for bringing in a fresh and sometimes challenging the status-quo, with a strategic approach delivering successful change management programmes and launching companies and products internationally that deliver results.

Contact information:

Geoffrey Hudson-Searle

Email: ghudsonsearle@gmail.com

Tel: +44 (0) 207 205 2490

LinkedIn: http://www.linkedin.com/in/geoffsearle

BeBee: https://www.bebee.com/bee/geoff-hudson-searle

Author of 'Meaningful Conversations'

https://meaningfulconversationsbook.com

Blog: www.freedomafterthesharks.com

CHAPTER VI

The Misunderstood Call

By Richard Kay

My story begins in Vilna, Lithuania where my father was born in 1912. In this small, Slavic village, his family was of the Jewish minority. The persecution of Jews had always been a major threat to their existence. By the time he was 17, he and his younger brother were able to escape further persecution by journeying to the United States. They made their home with relatives in New York and worked at various trades. My dad became a marine electrician and saw more opportunity to work in the shipyard. He met and married my mother and they moved to Mobile, Alabama in 1941 where he was able to work on military ships during World War II.

In 1943, I was born, the first of 5 children. Growing up as a Jew in the Deep South, I experienced many prejudices. Here again, we were very much a minority. My religious upbringing began with celebrating the Jewish holidays and learning more of my Jewish heritage. I studied Hebrew and read through many of the religious writings. By the time I was 13, I was Bar Mitzvah and confirmed in the Jewish faith. I loved my Jewish heritage and wanted to learn more. Most of my friends were Jewish but I did have a few who were Christians.

I graduated from high school in 1961 and thought that college was my best choice to find out what I wanted to do with the rest of my working life. There were several issues that I had to deal with while in school at the University of Nebraska. I was able to enroll there as an in-state student due to my father's job transfer to Lincoln, Nebraska. It was quite a different atmosphere of scholastic standing from my south Alabama high school. Although, I had maintained a B average, it only granted me probation for enrolment at Nebraska. I enrolled in Pre-Med because I thought I would become a doctor. This was similar to a child wanting to become a fireman but not uncommon as an aspiration for a young Jew.

There was yet another major issue in my life at that time. I had become an addicted gambler. As with many addictions, I didn't recognize the severity of gambling and its effect on my life. It became more important than school and continued to be my vice throughout my enlistment in the Marine Corps during the Viet Nam war. In all of this, I tried to remain loyal to my Jewish faith. It was hard to keep the laws of God. I failed miserably. After I got out of the Marine Corps, I got married and started a family. I had a respectable job and acceptance in my community but I was still a compulsive, addicted gambler.

No one needed to convince me of my sinful condition. I needed a solution to my gambling problem. God provided that solution through a course of events that led me to accept my Messiah. Jesus, the Messiah, paid the price for my sinful condition and replaced my insatiable desire to gamble with a hunger and thirst for a righteous relationship with Him. That began my new life in Him in April of 1969.

As time went on, I wanted to do more for God. I had witnessed to my friends and family and was able to participate in many areas of ministerial training. A book that I read titled "*Like A Mighty Wind*" about the Indonesian revival touched my inner desire to serve Him in a more committed way. My insatiable desire to gamble had been replaced by an unquenchable hunger for a deeper relationship with my Lord.

I became part of The Full Gospel Businessmen's Fellowship International, an organization founded by Demos Shakarian and served on the board of my local chapter. I appreciated the vision of Demos and his leaders. "*The mandate from God is we break the chains of bondage in the world. Our mandate is to destroy the isolation of loneliness, and link the world to God*" and "*It is our destiny to lift up Christ in every business center, every marketplace, every government center and university… every nation, city, town and crossroads of the world.*"

I began to write songs of praise and prayer. I was doing all this while holding down a full-time job in the insurance industry. I was spending much of my time visiting other believers and serving in the church Sunday school. The Lord was dealing with me about obedience. I was now the father of four children and I wanted to be able to spend time with them. In the insurance business, I had progressed to a District Manager position. I was responsible for training other agents and personal sales as well. My life was becoming very busy. In many ways I was more occupied with church life than family life. Being a good provider and trying to raise my family in a Godly manner was all that really mattered.

Each week I attended a prayer breakfast with some men from another church. It was a great time of fellowship and it was there that I learned more about *specific praying*. We saw God move in many miraculous ways and our devotion to God and one another became much stronger. Everything was moving on what seemed to be a well-charted course and the Lord impressed on me that He wanted more. That "*more*" translated into my decision to resign my position as a District Manager with American Bankers Life Assurance Co. and pursue what I felt was the call into the clergy.

My prayer breakfast partners were made aware and they confirmed that I should pursue the ministry. To make it possible, four of the senior members of the group committed to support my family while I entered bible school or seminary. This would allow me to follow God's leading without concern about how our bills would be paid. To put things in perspective, this was in 1972 and my annual earnings was about $20,000. This was quite a generous commitment for these men to make.

And so I began my search for the direction God would have me take. My application was sent to several seminaries expecting one or more of them to welcome me but that did not happen. I was invited to attend and audit classes of Fruitland Bible College, which I did but my application wasn't accepted. Each week, there were more applications and each week more refusals. It was quite an experience watching and waiting for God to open the right door. My church leadership was praying for me, my friends were praying for me but it seemed that either my timing was off or something was blocking me from entrance into a seminary.

After 9 months of applications and turndowns, I was frustrated and another brother in the Lord, Al Wittinghill and I were praying on my living room floor. We were the only people in the house at the time. Al and I had become close friends through attending the Billy Graham School of Evangelism in Atlanta, Georgia. We went as counselors at the crusade and as laymen for the evangelistic training. Anyway, Al and I were prostrated on my floor praying and I heard a familiar voice; this voice had been audibly heard by me one other time. The night I gave my life to the Lord, Jesus. He spoke to me in an assuring manner because I had also heard a much sterner and accusing voice. The one voice told me that I couldn't do this because I was a Jew. The other assuring voice, which was that of the Lord Jesus said, "*Yes, you can. I died for you.*".

Then the Lord's voice was clear and audible. He called me by name and this is what He said, "*Richard, you've given me everything in your life but the right to run your business. Now I want you go back into business, commit the business to me, I will run the business and that will be your ministry."* Well, I looked at Al to see if he heard anything and I told him what I had been told. We began praising God together for His answer to prayer even though I had no idea of what I was to do next.

From that time, things began to happen quickly. A phone call came from another insurance company, which asked me to meet with them the next day. I agreed and met with the Regional Vice President in Raleigh, NC. Remember, I had not drawn a paycheck for 9 months. My men's group was supporting me, and my family. This meeting resulted in an offer to become the State Director of North Carolina. When I asked about the salary, he stated that it would start at about $1,500 per week but that it would grow even more. You can imagine what was going through my mind. I thought when God moves He really moves! I asked the RVP if he would allow my wife and I to pray about the offer and I would get back to him with my answer. He agreed and I returned to Greensboro about 60 miles away.

When I got home I had barely entered the door and the phone rang. It was a Division Manager of American Bankers Life that I had given my resignation before. His name was Joe Beck and I only knew him from his success in the company. He asked me if I was still pursuing the *"ministry"* and I told him that I believe I was supposed to go back into business. He said that was good because he had a proposal he wanted to discuss with me. He wanted to start a new agency and wanted me to lead it. He would give me back my District Manager position and we would split the profits of the agency...but...he could only pay me $100 per week. Can you imagine the thought that I had with this offer? I told him I would pray about it and let him know. I have to confess; I felt that the other State Director position was certainly going to be the one God had opened for me.

I had been studying about Gideon and how God directed him to form the army He would use to defeat his enemies. I guess I could identify with Gideon and I asked God to show me how to put out a fleece. Now, this would not be placing lamb's wool outdoors in the night waiting for it to be damp with the morning dew or kept dry. No, this fleece would be accomplished by selecting scripture for each of the choices before me. You see, I felt that God answered prayer in one of three ways...Yes, No or Wait!

So that evening, my wife and I sat on opposite sides of the room, bibles in hand (unopened) and we asked God to give us three scriptures for each choice. These were written down individually and then we opened the bibles to reveal the verses.

Well, were we surprised at how accurate the word of God is for specific prayers! I will only give you a few examples here to illustrate. For the State Director's position, the scripture given was *"Beware of false prophets who come to you in sheep's clothing but inwardly are ravaging wolves"* Matthew 7:15; and two other similar answers. For Joe Beck's $100 per week offer, the first scripture was *"For who has despised the day of small things?"* Zechariah 4:10 and the scripture for Wait..... *"Now is the day of salvation"* 2 Corinthians 6:2. All the scriptures were clear.

I went to bed at peace with God's direction and the next day, I called both men. The State Director RVP was disappointed but said he understood. When I called Joe, I told him that I didn't really want to take his offer that I didn't even like him but that I believed this was what the Lord wanted me to do. The following day, I called each of the men who had been supporting my family and told them of my decision. They confirmed that I was truly following God's call. They also were relieved of their commitment to continue supporting my family.

The rest of the story is full of many wonderful and miraculous events that transpired in just this one step of committed obedience. For the business, we started with no agents and a new agency in January 1973. I did just what God told me to do. The business was completely in His hands and I was available for whatever He wanted me to do. Every morning, we met in the office for prayer. We began recruiting and training agents. Even though I had to go back to the very same insurance company that I had resigned position less than a year before, they were gracious and accepting. We prayed and asked God for favor in making and keeping insurance sales appointments. I would have a new agent trainee with me each time we covered an appointment. In the agency, God was answering prayers for our agents and their families. It was becoming obvious to other agencies that something was happening.

The Misunderstood Call

Here I will relate one such event. I was training a new agent, J. R. Smith, Jr. or "*Sonny*"; as he was known by his friends. We were in the middle of a presentation with a young couple about an educational savings plan for their children. Suddenly, I sensed the Lord saying, "*You're in the wrong book*". This led to ending the presentation and asking if they had a bible. They had a family bible that was an open fixture with dust and all. I also had a Gideon testament in my coat pocket. This was a wonderful night. The couple confessed to us that they were scheduled to go to the lawyer's office the next day to file for divorce. That night, God healed their marriage and the whole family was united in Him. But...no insurance other than eternal was accomplished that night. Sonny did not know quite what to make of this and wasn't sure he wanted to work with me anymore. My arrangement with a new agent was that when they worked with me, we would split my commission so they would earn 50% of my earnings. Well, that didn't seem to productive for Sonny Smith. He did hang in there and we continued to work together.

I would like to interject here that in actual hours of work in the office and field, resulted in about three days a week for me even though I was available anytime. What was happening on the other days and nights that were open were numerous opportunities to lead cottage prayer groups and bible studies. God was providing open doors and I was obedient to follow His lead.

Back to Sonny Smith; in the next week I had been given an unusual challenge to write a key man disability policy for the

Richard Kay

President and CEO of Air Balance Corporation. He had a heart condition and needed to have a reduction of his rating in order to take the policy. This was a million dollar face amount and the company was able to reduce his rating. When it came time to deliver the policy, Sonny was with me. We went to the home of the client and he invited us inside, offered us some iced tea and without reservation asked how did he make out his check. I thought that perhaps he would pay one month's premium, providing he accepted the policy. He wrote the check for the entire annual premium. We were in and out of his home in twenty minutes and Sonny Smith, because of our agreement, just earned several thousand dollars. When we got back to the car, he said, *"maybe there is something to this praying thing!"*.

Well, the next few months made records for our little agencies and our standing with the company. In the first quarter of 1973, we were the number one agency in new premium and I was the second highest paid District Manager in the entire company. *"Do not forsake small beginnings"* indeed. To God be the glory for the things He has done. Our agency had grown from zero to 42 licensed agents in North Carolina and Southwestern Virginia. We achieved Million Dollar Roundtable Lifetime Qualification.

More importantly, I have been privileged to pray with businessmen and we watched God move mightily in their lives. We've seen sick families healed, marriages put back together, and precious fruit being produced in our families as well. In retrospect, I have been asked to give my testimony at more churches and stood in more pulpits as a businessman committed to God than perhaps I would have ever done had I continued in the pursuit of the call to the clergy.

Now many years later and many business ventures where God has continued to show His faithfulness, I have been blessed to write what He has given me in the form of three books and over 100 songs. I have seen our prayers answered for others and have been able to be used of God in ways I would not have thought humanly possible. Now, at 76 years of age and blessed with good health, my wife and I enjoy being able to continue giving and being available where ever God leads.

In Colossians 2:9-10, we read

9 "For in Him dwells all the fullness
of the Godhead bodily;
10 and you are complete in Him,
who is the head of all principality and power."

I'm just one of God's works being completed, *a sinner saved by His grace*, given eternal life in Him.

Further in 2 Corinthians 5:18-21

18 "Now all things are of God, who has
reconciled us to Himself through Jesus Christ,
and has given us the ministry of reconciliation,
19 that is, that God was in Christ reconciling the
world to Himself, not [a]imputing their
trespasses to them, and has committed to
us the word of reconciliation.
20 Now then, we are ambassadors for Christ, as
though God were pleading through us:
we implore you on Christ's behalf,
be reconciled to God.
21 For He made Him who knew no sin to be sin
for us, that we might become the
righteousness of God in Him".

It is my prayer that through this story of God's grace, mercy and forgiveness, others will identify the misunderstood call on their lives and obediently follow in commitment to Him.

Richard Kay | Bio

Richard Kay has had a diverse career history in the financial service industry. After studying business at the University of Nebraska and the University of Maryland, he served in the United States Marine Corps during the Vietnam War. Upon being honorably discharged, he began working in various sectors of business. Being raised as a Jew, he accepted the Messiah through a course of events that led to a Billy Graham Crusade in 1969.

He was called into "*marketplace ministry*" before many understood how believers can be used of God perhaps even more in business than in the pulpit. Richard served as an officer in the Full Gospel Business Men's Fellowship International organization and an active Gideon. His dedication and devotion to help others is noted in all aspects of his personal and business life.

He is an ordained minister and has served the church for the past 50 years. He is on the Board of Directors and is the Treasurer of two non-profit, ministries in the USA and India. Richard is the international spokesman of Reflections On The Word, a daily ministry radio broadcast and the author of several books including "*What it Means To Be A Jew*"; "*War and Victory, The Christian Fight of Faith*" and the latest eBook "*Three Days After Calvary*".

He and his wife, Ellie, have been members of New Life Church in Virginia since 1991. They live in Chesapeake, where they enjoy ministry, traveling and the ability to give back to the community.

CHAPTER VII

Go Serve Big!

You Will Never Be Second
When You Put Others First

By Rudy Lira Kusuma

By committing to a common purpose and shared values, we can adopt a way of doing business that allows the ownership, the staff team members, the agents, customers and clients – to win.

Company: Your Home Sold Guaranteed Realty

Our Vision: To Be The Best Place to Work, Buy and Sell Real Estate in California!

Our Mission: To Help You Achieve Your Hearts Desire

Our Core Commitments: Five Core Value Commitments to Each Other, Our Clients and Our Community!

- Second Mile Service
- Empower and Inspire Others
- Results Driven
- Value Relationships by Expressing Gratitude
- Embrace Continual Improvement

Through a commitment to Second Mile Service, Empowering and Inspiring Others, Being Results Driven, Valuing Relationships by Expressing Gratitude, and Embracing Continual Improvement, our company will endeavor to be the best place to work for our team members, the best place to buy and sell real estate for our clients, be the best stewards for our shareholders, and give our best to our community.

Second Mile Service

Matthew 5:41

41 Whoever compels you to go one mile,
go with him two.

Second mile service has its roots all the way back in first-century Palestine. The Romans had conquered most of the Mediterranean world. One of the marvels of their conquest was a vast system of super highways that they had built for travel to and from their conquered territories. There were more than fifty thousand miles of these Roman roads throughout the Empire. At each single mile was a stone marker. These mile markers pointed directions, determined the distance to the next town as well as to Rome itself, and warned of dangers that might lie ahead. Hence the common phrase *"All roads lead to Rome"*.

By law, a Roman citizen or soldier could compel a subject from one of the conquered lands to carry his backpack, or load, for him for one mile, but one mile only. Jesus, as he was preaching His famous Sermon on the Mount said, "*Whoever compels you to go one mile, go with him two*".

Can you imagine the bombshell this must have been as it fell upon the ears of those under Roman occupation that were listening to His sermon? Jesus called upon His hearers to do what was required of them — and then some.

What is it that separates some from others in athletics or education or business or the arts, or in any endeavor? It is their drive to do more than is expected or required.

When focusing on the second mile, many forget there are two miles in play here. The first is a mandated mile; the second is a miracle mile.

There is a Mandated Mile Motivated By Law

The first mile is simply what is required of us. The first mile is always the hardest though. Ask the distance runner. The second wind never kicks in on the first mile. The truth is, it is not as easy to enjoy the things we have to do as it is to enjoy the things we want to do.

When an agent sells a home many companies celebrate as if this is some accomplishment. They send post cards out saying, "*Hey look what I did, I sold a house!*" But isn't this what IS required of us? Spiking the football, putting on the jacket or ringing the bell when the agent sells a house - is expected by the client. Isn't that what you do, sell houses?

I think the reason agents celebrate it is because it's tough to get started on the first mile. Ask any first-century Jew under Roman rule. The first mile interrupts your schedule when you are compelled to perform it. It causes you to swallow your own pride and bear an extra burden. Likewise, often the most difficult part is getting started on the first mile. This is true with almost everything in life, with exercise programs, dieting, and scores of other disciplines. In fact, many try to play leapfrog with Matthew 5:41. That is, they want to enjoy the little extras of the second mile, but they do not want to deal with the requirements of the first mile.

There can be no second mile service without going the first mile.

There Is a Second Mile Motivated by Love of Others

It is this mile that separates certain individuals from others. The second mile is only made possible by being obedient to the first mile. The second mile has a way of brightening our own road. Think about it. Imagine a first-century boy working at his trade. A Roman soldier comes by, calls to him, and demands that he carry his backpack for one mile down the road. Now, this command interrupts the lad's whole day and takes him away from his work. But he has no choice. However, this boy is a second-miler. They approach the one-mile marker and instead of putting down the pack, spitting on the ground, and marching back home, he volunteers to go an extra mile with the soldier. That sort of thing changes people. That sort of service is contagious. That sort of person changes lives.

Someone who journeys on the second mile also has a way of lightening the load of those around them. One cannot travel the second mile without influencing others. It only takes one second-miler in a home to change the entire environment. It only takes one second-miler on a team or in the office to do the same.

Now that we have clear understanding of what Second Mile Service is, let's examine our commitment to Our Clients, Each Other, The Stakeholders and Our Community with Second Mile Service.

For Our Clients We are Committed to Exceeding Expectations and Will Never Cut Corners.

Most real estate agents, not all but most, admit they got into real estate because they believed they could make more money and be their own boss. It is true that a successful agent will do well financially and yes an agent as an independent contractor and is in charge of their own schedule. But somewhere along the way those that understand second mile service come to believe their business is not for them, it is for others.

Imagine that as an agent your commission checks can't be cashed to pay any of your bills. They are simply a measuring stick and offer no financial value. Instead, you can only pay your bills, eat and sleep indoors with Referrals, Five Star Reviews, and Repeat Business. If this were true, would you do things differently? Would you build your business and conduct your business differently in order to ensure service went well beyond just getting a commission check? Of course you would.

Exceeding clients' expectations has to be built into the very fabric of the business from the peoples mind set to the systems to the culture. Anything short would be cutting corners.

Second Mile Service for Our People Means Making it Easy to Over Deliver!

Getting customers and taking care of them is hard enough as it is. It does not need to be made harder by complex business methods or dysfunction among company departments and levels. Leading edge technology and clarity of core processes are an integral part of the SYSTEM at Your Home Sold Guaranteed Realty. Approaching each day with an attitude of good enough never translates into a steady look at questioning the status quo, keeping us dedicated to helping the great people at this historic company over deliver!

The company was founded by a super successful real estate agent, Rudy Lira Kusuma. In fact, when Rudy L. Kusuma hired the very first accountant, Rudy told them their *"#1 priority was to make sure the agent got their money the instant a closing takes place, after all it's their money... not ours!"*

Nothing against industry brokers, it's just that the perspective and lens all things are done by and seen thru at Your Home Sold Guaranteed Realty is that of the agent and what will make it easier for them to over deliver great service to our clients.

After all, we (the leadership team at Your Home Sold Guaranteed Realty) have been there and done that and successfully taught many others how to do it (establish a super profitable real estate sales team business).

For Our Stakeholders, Second Mile Service Means Being Exceptional Stewards of the Brand and Revenue.

We have the #1 Real Estate Business Building System in history with Coaching and Training done by some of the top real estate agents in history. *To whom much is given much is required.*

A great way to look at this would be to look at one of the greatest stories ever told by the greatest leader in history; the parable of the talents.

The *"Parable of the Talents"*, in Matthew 25:14–30 tells of a master who was leaving his house to travel, and, before leaving, entrusted his property to his servants. According to the abilities of each man, one servant received five talents, the second servant received two talents, and the third servant received one talent. The property entrusted to the three servants was worth 8 talents, where a talent was a significant amount of money. Upon returning home, after a long absence, the master asks his three servants for an account of the talents he entrusted to them. The first and the second servants explain that they each put their talents to work, and have doubled the value of the property with which they were entrusted; each servant was rewarded:

Matthew 25:23

²³ His master said to him, 'Well done good and faithful servant. You have been faithful over a little; I will set you over much. Enter into the joy of your master.'

The third servant, however, had merely hidden his talent, had buried it in the ground, and was punished by his master:

Matthew 25:24-30

[24] *"Then the one who had received the one talent came and said, 'Sir, I knew that you were a hard man, harvesting where you did not sow, and gathering where you did not scatter seed,* [25] *so I was afraid, and I went and hid your talent in the ground. See, you have what is yours.'* [26] *But his master answered, 'Evil and lazy servant! So you knew that I harvest where I didn't sow and gather where I didn't scatter?* [27] *Then you should have deposited my money with the bankers, and on my return I would have received my money back with interest!* [28] *Therefore take the talent from him and give it to the one who has ten.* [29] *For the one who has will be given more, and he will have more than enough. But the one who does not have, even what he has will be taken from him.*

*[30] And throw that worthless slave into the outer
darkness, where there will be weeping
and gnashing of teeth.'"*

Accountability is something many in our world want no part of. The most successful though know they are owed nothing, but owe giving their all every day to others, especially to those that entrust them with extreme value. Deliver MORE value than what is/was/will be received = over deliver.

For Our Community, We Will Walk the Walk and Talk the Talk on Going the Extra Mile.

Everyone has a story. It's likely that everyone is or has or will go through a hard time of some kind. In our world today though many walk thru it as if they are the only ones that matter. It's as if they own the road and everyone else is in their way. How hard is it to say thank you, hold the door open for someone or allow a car to have the gap in front of you? Right, not hard. *Selfless vs selfish.* When you study successful people in history, you will discover that at some point along their path people began to do business with them not so much for what they did, but for who they were.

Second mile service doesn't start and end with a real estate transaction; it is a way of life. It is essentially who you are.

"A community loves on those who love on their community"

— Dr. Ike Reighard.

Second Mile Service Commitments

- Exceed our client's expectations and never cut corners.
- Make it easy for everyone in the company to deliver second mile service!
- Be exceptional stewards of revenue for Shareholders.
- Walk the walk and talk the talk of going the extra mile in the Community.

Rudy Lira Kusuma | Bio

Rudy L. Kusuma is the Chief Executive of Your Home Sold Guaranteed Realty and the Managing Director of TEAM NUVISION, #1 Real Estate Sales Team in California. In addition, Your Home Sold Guaranteed Realty has been named for multiple years in a row as INC 5000 Fastest Growing Private Company in America, as well as ranked Top 100 Fastest Growing

Private Company in Los Angeles as published by The Los Angeles Business Journal.

Rudy and his team have served over 5000 families, and negotiated over a billion dollars in real estate transactions. He has been awarded multiple top producers awards, including The Five Star Real Estate Professional Award as published in the Los Angeles Magazine, and named as one of America's Best Real Estate Agents as published in the Wall Street Journal.

As a philanthropist, Rudy is on a mission to raise $100,000 for the Children's Hospital in downtown Los Angeles. For every house that his team sells, Rudy and his team are donating a portion of their income to the Children's Hospital. Not only home sellers benefit from his team award winning service, but they donate a substantial portion of their income on every home sale to help the local children in the community.

Rudy provides numerous public resources regarding how to buy and sell real estate in today's real estate market. His expert advice have been published by community newspapers, including: Indonesia Media, Mid Valley News, Temple City Life, Temple City Tribune, Arcadia Weekly, Monrovia Weekly, El Monte Examiner, San Gabriel Sun, Duarte Dispatch, Rosemead Reader, Azusa Beacon, and Around Alhambra Newspapers.

Rudy L. Kusuma lives in Temple City with his wife and two sons. He can be reached online at: www.YourHomeSoldGuaranteedInc.com

or by telephone at (626) 789-0159

Rudy Lira Kusuma California Real Estate Broker License 01820322

CHAPTER VIII

Seeds Of Adversity:
Blessings In Disguise
By Chuck Bolena

Jim Rohn talks about *'the day that turns your life around.'* My day was November 2014 and I never could have imagined what was coming my way – a true blessing in disguise, and to think I almost missed it.

Like many a day, I would stop at a local coffee shop in the morning and grab my coffee, bagel or baked good(s), and get on the road to make my sales calls for the day. I was in medical sales and worked for a very small company at the time. This particular morning I saw a gentleman sitting at a table when I entered. He was by himself and I knew him only well enough to say *'Hi,'* so I did. His name is Jim Shorkey and he is well known in Western Pennsylvania for his ownership and incredible growth of the Jim Shorkey Family Auto Group. At the time, he owned six dealerships in total. I greeted him and introduced myself, telling him how I had met him once or twice before. We talked briefly and I went about my business grabbing breakfast and getting on the road. Before I left the coffee shop, Jim approached me and asked for a business card. I gave him one, thinking nothing about what that short interaction would mean for me moving forward.

How many times have you had the opportunity to do or say something nice for someone and didn't? You see someone with a really nice jacket or dress on, a waitress that presents with a great attitude and sense of service that exceeds your expectation, a young mom sitting across from you at a restaurant with her young children choosing to engage them in conversation and laughing at their jokes instead of flipping through her cell phone, or you see a man dressed nicely standing on the side of the road next to his car with a flat tire.

Do you comment on the jacket or dress? Do you recognize the waitress? Do you compliment the mom? Do you stop and help the gentleman on the side of the road?

I have stepped out of my comfort zone and acted on each of the scenarios listed above. I didn't always act this way. I would talk myself out of it and miss the chance to bless someone when presented the opportunity. Mel Robbins talks about the 5-second Rule and I started using it. I would see an opportunity and know that if I didn't act within 5 seconds, I'd miss my chance and do nothing, often regretting my decision. I decided my one act of kindness might very well be the only kindness that person receives that day. I now (nine times out of 10) step up and act. I have a daily discipline in my journal labeled 'RAK' which stands for Random Act of Kindness. I want to perform a RAK at least once every day. Not only does it bless the person I show kindness to, but it also blesses me too as their response is always kindness in return.

So my RAK with Jim turned into a phone call not long after we crossed paths, asking if we could meet for coffee. He indicated that he was no longer in the car business; he retired and handed the business over to his four children, and was doing something different and wanted to share it with me. Intrigued only by the fact that it was Jim who wanted to meet me, I agreed and our first meeting was December 9th, 2014.

He proceeded to tell me that he started a coaching and mentoring company and wanted to help others become successful as well. Jim's success didn't come easy and without a struggle. His father passed in 1996 and Jim was now in charge. Due to his admitted ego and a desire to grow his father's family run business bigger and better than ever, was facing bankruptcy two years later. His overconfident efforts proved to be disastrous and he needed to do something about his struggling business, and fast.

Jim was already studying personal development books and listening to recordings from Bryan Tracy and the like. He had read Napoleon Hill's book, *Think and Grow Rich*, but failed to implement anything he studied, until this point in his life. He had no choice. His mom, siblings, and others were relying on him to keep the business afloat. He began implementing the principles presented by Napoleon Hill's book and saw the needle moving. He persisted and saw stronger results. He kept reading *Think and Grow Rich*, implementing the concepts, adapting his strategy and

141

getting stronger and stronger results. He grew that one dealership, selling 800 new and used cars a year and having 40 employees, to a total of 6 dealerships with 400 employees, selling close to 8,000 cars a year. Today, the family-run business now totals nine dealerships across Western Pennsylvania and into Ohio, and their success is astronomical. Jim attributes all of his success to the implementation of the principles in *Think and Grow Rich*. He continues to read this book and has exceeded 140 total reads to date, cover to cover, and plans on reading it again and again and again. When something seems to work and work well, when do you decide to stop? You don't!

As much as Jim's presentation was compelling to me when we met, I had no interest in being coached nor did I have the time I was too new with a small company and the idea of digging up my life to reevaluate and make changes didn't interest me at the time. I was focused on my sales growth and everything else took a back seat: my health, my finances, even my marriage and family to a degree. There are times where certain things take priority, and my new role had to be a top priority over everything else – at least that was my thinking at the time. I invested a lot of time into my role and felt Jim couldn't help in an industry that his success didn't take place in. How can his success in the automobile industry help me in the medical device industry? The answer amazed me.

We met two more times, December 15th, and then finally on December 17th, before I agreed to be coached by Jim. I believe my decision had more to do with his skill as a car salesman and less to do with my willingness to spend the money or invest the time. Either way, this decision pushed me further into the life-changing event that was playing out and I had no clue what was happening.

I believe people are placed in your life for various reasons - sometimes for a reason, sometimes for a season of your life, and sometimes for a lifetime. I believe my meeting Jim was for a reason, and it's turning into a lifetime.

I began the coaching program with Jim in January 2015. He was working with 10-15 other clients, hosting weekly group meetings as well as one-on-one sessions to help each client move along their journey.

I admit, I enjoyed the readings and questions that helped me get focused on what I wanted in life as well as a reality check of where my life was. It wasn't easy going through this awakening, but it was necessary. Few people stop and look in the mirror at their life. If done properly, it's a humbling experience. You'll see things that you don't want to see. You'll identify success, but will also dig up failures that you won't want to relive. This is a necessary process to discover where your life is and where you desire to go. I began to appreciate the awareness and subtle changes I was making in such a short amount of time.

I enjoyed the group sessions and found myself engaging with others on the various topics discussed. I would challenge them on different things discussed and help them open their mind's eye to see things differently. The material made sense to me and I was beginning to view my life differently.

This was all happening to me at the age of 48 for a reason. God only gives us what we can handle (sometimes it appears as if he's giving us more then we can handle). If presented this information earlier in my life, or by someone different, I don't believe I would be where I am now, as I would have rejected this concept and offer in the years past. I am blessed by the turn of events and I'm thankful for the growth I have experienced so far, and excited about where I'm going.

I truly believe God grants us more talent and ability than we can use in a lifetime. Our gift to God is to use as much of that talent and ability we can in our lifetime. Opportunities like this allow us to grow stronger so we can apply those talents and gifts more and more, and in doing so, everyone wins.

Make no mistake, I didn't get rich quick, lose 40 pounds, improve my health and marriage, etc., etc. This was a learning and growing process; an awakening of who I was compared to who I wanted to be. I began implementing the changes in my life and I began seeing results with my sales. This was my focus and my number one goal at the time.

Two things happened that I didn't expect: First, my sales numbers skyrocketed and I had a three-fold increase in results that I never expected. The second unanticipated thing that happened was Jim asking me to partner with him in his company, Results from Thinking. I was blown away by both outcomes and was thrilled at the opportunity of helping people directly in a similar role that Jim did for me.

Seeds Of Adversity:
Blessings In Disguise

When I was in the Air Force (1992-2000), I had the opportunity to earn a Master's Degree in Counseling and Development from Montana State University – Northern. I loved the program. It was my first 4.0 GPA ever and I wanted to open a counseling practice one day. My last assignment in the Air Force was as an Assistant Professor of Aerospace Studies at Penn State University in the Air Force ROTC Program. I taught the senior class and held several other roles within the program to help facilitate the training and education of future Air Force Officers. I anticipated taking a few remaining courses to become licensed in Pennsylvania as a counselor, but at the time, Pennsylvania did not recognize licensed counselors and that dream came to a halt. After my assignment at Penn State, I chose to step away from the military and relocate back where my wife and I grew up to raise our kids. I entered the pharmaceutical Industry in 2000 and eventually moved to medical sales, and to the role I had when I met Jim.

Jim's proposal would allow me the opportunity to fulfill my passion of helping others overcome life's challenges. I was excited at the opportunity; yet fearful of the drastic changes it would have on my family and my career. I had 15 years in the medical sales industry and this would be a dramatic shift to take. After about two weeks of thinking it through and talking with my wife on this decision, she encouraged me to do it, and I did.

I gave notice and was working with Jim full-time shortly after making the decision. This was scary as I had to take a chance to make a change - doing something like this is scary for most anyone. It's exactly the thing that keeps people right where they are, never pursuing joy and happiness in life. Regardless of the difficulty in making such a drastic change in careers, this proved to be one of the best decisions I've made – another turning point in my life as a result of approaching Jim in a coffee shop in November 2014. Not only was I doing what I believed was my calling of helping others more directly, but I was also learning the power of mindset and the importance of Napoleon Hill's message of *'taking possession of one's own mind and directing it to ends of one's own choosing.'* This was changing who I was and how I interacted with my world in a very positive way. I was becoming better as I helped others become better. What a blessing in disguise! None of this would have happened unless I jumped and took a leap of faith towards my passion for serving and helping others. Too many times we let fear keep us from taking the chances needed to grow and do what I believe we were meant to do.

Here's what I learned through all this: my dramatic improvement in my sales had less to do with everything I complained about (lack of coverage by insurance companies, the competition outnumbering me six to one or more, poor marketing resources, limited supplies, poor leadership, and direction, etc.) and everything to do with me and how I handled the circumstances I faced - big difference in mindset, right?

It was so easy to play the blame game and be a victim. I learned that my actions had more impact on my future outcomes regardless of who was at fault or what adversities came my way.

Seeds Of Adversity:
Blessings In Disguise

When I chose to work from the '*inside out*' instead of an '*outside-in*' perspective (also known as an Internal Locus of Control vs. an External Locus of control) I had a breakthrough. I empowered myself and was able to regain control in areas of my life that I lacked control over. There are way too many people living the blame game and not taking control of their own life and circumstances, and I did the same thing for way too long. It was easy to do and it served me initially, or so I thought. We all are conditioned to be who we currently are and do what we currently do – good and bad. When bad habits give us results that fall short of our potential and make us unhappy, it's time to take a serious look at our life and make a change once and for all.

This new career change and discovery of the power of mindset was liberating and exciting, but I had no idea how this would serve me, possibly even save my life, as I was about to be faced with the biggest health challenge ever. Something that would impact my wife, my kids, my family and friends, and the work I was destined to do.

Not long after my diagnosis in April 2018, I was talking with Jim and told him that had I received this diagnosis prior to meeting him, I think I would have had a horrible time accepting the fact that I was diagnosed with stage iii colon *canser* (I deliberately minimized the words and even misspelled it to show a lack of respect for this invasive disease!).

Two factors played a role here: first is my faith and belief in my Creator. I was not always a strong Christian as my earlier years

I don't believe I had much faith or belief in God. My faith had become stronger as I matured, but I believe it gained strength over the last year – interesting, huh?

Most people make life-altering changes in their life in one of two ways: One is by choice and through repetition, replacing bad habits with good ones. The other is after an emotional impact happens, altering life instantly. A loss of a loved one, a near-death experience, or even a life-threatening medical diagnosis such as cancer. One allows you to make changes in the state of joy and happiness, the other in the state of misery and depression. If you had a choice, which would you choose?

The second factor that played a role following my diagnosis is my four years of training and understanding of the power of the mind and the ability to minimize the impact the outside world has over my thought process - ultimately my life. A quote I've used time and again during this period of my life is, "*In every adversity is the seed of equal or greater opportunity, or blessings.*" This simple statement has altered my perspective on my diagnosis as well as the rest of my life.

It's amazing how people will struggle to go through life in the state of fear and worry, focused on that which brings them discomfort or heartache. In doing so, they miss the opportunity or blessings placed there (I believe by God) and never know the true joy that could come out of this period of their life. I have been given the gift of foresight and the ability to realize just how short and fragile life can be. This experience has given me the vision to

Seeds Of Adversity:
Blessings In Disguise

live without stress, see hidden opportunities, say what I'm thinking, do what I desire, and feel blessed and honored to have another day on this earth to live my calling of blessing more an more people by the work I do, not to mention spending time with the people I love and are important to me.

I believe faith in God and faith in self (we are created in His image) is critical to understanding and thriving in a world set with pitfalls, struggles, and death. The concept of leaving your faith *'at the door'* when you don your professional cap because there's a societal belief that *'there's no place for religion in the workplace,'* is foolish and doesn't allow yourself to live authentically, honestly, sincerely, and with passion and humility.

Chick-fil-a has always impressed me on how they train their employees. The management entrusts their employees at all levels with the authority to resolve customer issues, empower them with a sense of service, authentic teamwork, and respect, and honor the Sabbath in spite of lost revenue while other businesses continue on 24 hours a day, seven days a week, and often 365 days a years. As an employee of Chic-fil-a, you don't have to be a Christian, but you need to honor and live up to the professional standards of humility, compassion, and care for all guest and colleagues. That is the power of faith in business and living the values authentically.

How do you live out your faith in business? How do you handle adversity when it happens? Are you happy with the results you're producing?

It's never too late to do the right thing. It's never too late to live your life by design instead of by chance; to change your habits to generate the desired results. I've worked with a 12-year-old as well as a 62-year-old in my coaching business and the message and actions needed are still the same.

You can make the necessary changes in life under the shadows of adversity or you can choose to take action now, with an Internal Locus of Control, and generate the outcomes you want. Stop settling. Stop adhering to the views and opinions of other people.

Live your life the way you want, allowing your faith to shine regardless of your circumstances, and choose to seek the seeds left behind in the aftermath of adversities! You'll be amazed at the difference these subtle changes make in your life!

Chuck Bolena | Bio

Chuck Bolena, M.Ed., is a Certified John Maxwell Mindset Development Coach, Speaker, Amazon #1 Best Selling Author, Maxwell DISC Behavioral Analyst, and President of Results from Thinking. He holds a Master's Degree in Counseling and Development and has a successful and diverse, 23 year background in pharmaceutical sales, medical sales, mid-level management and military leadership as an Air Force Officer. His passion is to help inspire others to have more, do more, and be more in life. He can be reached at chuckbolena@gmail.com

CHAPTER IX

First Step Faith

By Kevin V. Riles

Let me start with an honest statement to set the tone of what I am about to tell you. When John Wesley Clayton, the editor and publisher of this book and Taft Mohair, one of my fellow contributing authors, asked me to contribute a chapter, I was reluctant at first. Why? As of the writing of this chapter, I felt like I was at a faith crossroads. I thought it was not a particularly good time for me to be writing a chapter in a book entitled *God in Business: Faith is the Deciding Factor*. So here I am on a Sunday evening writing this chapter literally the day before it's due after asking John for an extension. Why would I, Kevin Riles, a licensed minister, a Young Adult Sunday School Teacher, a 20+ year business owner, a preacher's kid be having a faith crisis at 45 years old? It doesn't make logical sense, but it's true. I have been lukewarm in the faith category for some time now.

If you look at my business and professional resume (inserted within this book as an exhibit of Blessings, not Hubris), you would think that someone who has accomplished so much and is a known Christian, could never have lukewarm faith. Yes, all of us go through moments where we question if God's faith applies to us. The key word in that sentence is MOMENT. That's a natural part of our Christian walk. Everyone has Moments. There are numerous stories throughout the Bible, new and Old Testament, where the Faith Moments crop up. Moments are one thing, but I've been in a season of lukewarm faith. I had been in such a faith funk that I was just minutes from emailing the publisher to withdraw as a contributing writer. You see; it's hard to be reflective about faith. It's difficult to admit to those who will read this book that your faith crisis was real and is real. After all, this is a motivational book, an inspirational book. I know this without even having seen my fellow contributing author's chapters.

So I sit here, at my kitchen table, typing with no particular plan but having the overwhelming feeling that I owe it to you to tell my story and be unapologetically truthful with you about where I have been and where I hope to go. I want to tell you that though I have been "*in the valley of death*" in terms of faith, **I still believe!** A mustard seed of faith still exists within me. I want that seed to grow much higher in me than it is now, but it's there.

If you, like me, are having a lukewarm faith season, walk with me as I lay bare to you my Business & Life Journey and where it can inform you and me. I do fundamentally believe that our past informs our future. To that end, these are the stories I will look to break out of my lukewarm faith system.

I've always wanted to be an entrepreneur. The first "*business*" I can remember starting was selling candy. I would purchase bulk candy, blow pops to be exact, and sell them for a profit at school and out of the front door of my house. It was going pretty good until two things happened. My logistics route to Sam's Wholesale Club was cut off by my mother being too busy to get me there. The other problem that ultimately was the death nail was that my landlord didn't like all of the neighborhood kids marking up her white front door by knocking on it. NOTE: The Logistics Driver and the Landlord are the same people: My Mother! True Story!

So as you can see, entrepreneurship is deep within my genetic code. Fast forward to the year 2001, where I first remember faith becoming something I was aware of in terms of business. After college, I was recruited and hired by the largest oil company in the world. I was overjoyed to receive multiple offers coming out of college but was even happier that this company based in my hometown of Houston, TX, extended an offer. I worked there from 1995 to 2000. Although I did very well there in terms of performance and was well liked, I HATED IT! I was just not cut out for corporate life. I would get physically sick on Sunday nights in anticipation of having to go to work Monday morning. At the same time of having these feelings, I decided to purchase my first house. I had always believed that real estate was the key to wealth, and so at 25 years old, I wanted to begin my wealth journey. I was blessed to meet another engineer who had his real estate license. He convinced me to purchase a duplex so that I could live in one unit and rent out the other, thereby letting the tenant pay my mortgage. It was genius, and I did it. Going through that process and watching him be an engineer by day and a real estate agent by night inspired me. So I decided to do the same thing. I got my real estate license. I would go to work during the day as an engineer and assist friends and family in the evenings with their real estate needs. I LOVED IT! I loved helping people! I loved teaching people! Best of all, I was good at it.

My misery continued in corporate life for the next few years. The company paid for my MBA in Finance, and upon received that degree, I was recruited by another company with a 60% pay raise. I immediately jumped at the chance for more money and more responsibility but guess what? I HATED IT, as well. Again, I was just not cut out for corporate life. By this time, my *"side"* real estate business was flourishing. I found myself spending more and more time practicing real estate than doing anything else. I will never forget one Monday morning when I arrived at work; the new company I worked for called the entire workforce into a conference room. They proceeded to tell us that the company was closing and everyone would be laid off. You would think based on me HATING my job that I would have been excited by the prospects of freedom, but I was not. I was terrified. You see, I just had gotten married a few years earlier. My wife, Cher, and I had just purchased a new home, and therefore, life and bills were a very real thing for me at the time. I was

PETRIFIED! I went home that evening worried and panicked. What was I going to do? How could I support my burgeoning family? How would I pay my mortgage? What about Benefits?

A STATEMENT ON FAITH: As I write this and take a pause on the story, I reflect on that time in my life and realize that DOUBT & ANXIETY ALWAYS PRECEDES A FAITH MOMENT! Significant doubt and anxiety are always present before we put our faith to work. I would argue that uncertainty and fear are an essential starting point for us to realize the power of God! These questions of What, How, When, and How Much are apart of our human experience. The answers to those questions are apart of our God experience. The Bible talks about the Fruits of the Spirit (Galatians 5: 22-23). The byproduct of walking in the spirit is love, joy, peace, patience, kindness, goodness, faithfulness, gentleness, and self-control. As human creatures, we crave all of these virtues. I can tell you that of these nine fruits, the one I desire the most at that time of my life was peace. Doubt and Anxiety were blocking me from my peace. Therefore, in my mind, I was not walking in the spirit. Again another time where I was at a faith crossroads!

Fast forward to the weekend after being informed I along with all of my co-workers would be laid off. I was sitting in my home office on my computer. There was this new company and website called Monster.com (remember it was 2001). I had heard a few friends who had good luck finding jobs on Monster.com, so I decided to give it a try. I spent an hour loading and formatting my resume in their system before starting my job search. As I scrolled the numerous job offerings in my field, I began to get that same feeling I got on Sunday nights before heading into work: PANIC, DEPRESSION, RESENTMENT, ANGER! As I sat back in my chair to calm my nerves, my eyes caught the whiteboard I had in my office with a list of the real estate transactions I was working on. I had always kept a record of deals that I was working on so that I would know who I was working with, what stage of the process we were in, and how many and when closings were occurring. As I looked at the list, I realized that I had enough deals going that if they closed when they were supposed to, I was going to make as much as 50% of my current salary in the next two months! Wow! At that moment, God gave me the wisdom to ask this question: WHY ARE YOU LOOKING FOR ANOTHER JOB? WHY ARE YOU LOOKING FOR ANOTHER JOB YOU WILL HATE WHEN I'VE GIVEN YOU ALL THAT YOU NEED AND WANT?!?!

That question would forever change the course of my life. However, would I act on it? Here comes the test: WOULD I TAKE THE FIRST STEP? WOULD I HAVE THE FAITH TO STRIKE OUT ON MY OWN? Are you at a crossroads in your life at the moment? Are you wondering what to do in terms of leaving a "*safe job*" and stepping out on your own? Do you have doubt and anxiety about taking THAT FIRST STEP? I am here to tell you that YOU HAVE TO TAKE THE FIRST STEP! My story informs me that the first step is the hardest to take! In the days between being laid off and starting my real estate company, I anguished over what to do. My faith was tested by doubt, questions, and anxiety, but let me tell you that my faith was also informed by what GOD put in my spirit and my genetics.

God allowed me to realize that all my life's journey had prepared me to take MY FIRST STEP! Selling candy when I was younger taught me about business, logistics, and landlords (smile)! Purchasing my first home taught me about real estate, marketing, location, and wealth building. Working in Corporate America taught me professionalism, project management, system, and teamwork. The more and more I thought about taking the first step to Entrepreneurship, the more I was emboldened with Faith because God had been preparing me all along! I know that's true for you as well. God has been preparing you for your destiny since before you were born. *"Before I formed you in the womb, I knew you!"*(Jeremiah 1:5) So you see having FIRST STEP FAITH is easy! God has preordained your direction! You don't have to worry! You don't have to doubt it! You already have FIRST STEP FAITH!

I am pleased to inform you that I took that first step and started my real estate company. Now some 20 plus years later I have had a life that I couldn't have imagined. Yes, I have made money and been able to support my family. My journey has not been without pitfalls. The years of 2006-2008 during the US financial crisis almost broke me financially and spiritually. I had to employ NEXT STEP FAITH to get through that, but I survived.

My company grew from just me in my home office to me having a staff of 4 and over 25 plus agents working with me. I received government contracts to sell properties and sold over 3500 homes. I transitioned to commercial real estate in the last 10 years and paired down my staff as I had to exercise KNOW THYSELF FAITH so that I could be truly happy within my own company and within myself. I can report to you as of the time of this writing in 2019, that 2018 was the best business year of my 20 plus year career in real estate. I was the happiest, I made the most money, and I had the best balance of home and work life EVER!

None of the above would have been possible without exercising FIRST STEP FAITH! I will be honest with you, writing this chapter has allowed me to see the light of faith peak through the clouds of despair. As you remember from the beginning, I have been in a faith funk. I realize in writing this now that I (and you as well) need to take time to remember our FIRST STEP FAITH moments! I know that we all get SPIRITUAL AMNESIA! We forget what God has done for us. We must not forget as our faith stories of the past, inform our faith crisis of the future. The same Faith we needed to start is the same faith we need to continue. Therefore, I can report to you that 2300 words into this chapter, I see the faith light, and it's all because I was asked to contribute to this book! How awesome is God to give me this opportunity where I was asked to help others, and I end up helping myself in the process!

So, therefore, I ask those who read this not to despair if they are having faith issues. You are not alone. All of us, from preachers to teachers, business owners to writers, deal with lingering faith issues. It's apart of life's journey. The next time you are going through it, just remember your FIRST STEP FAITH! It will Guide you through!

Selah....

KEVIN V. RILES | Bio

ENTREPRENEUR AND MOTIVATIONAL
SPEAKER

Kevin V. Riles serves as President and CEO of Kevin Riles Commercial-A Commercial Real Estate Services and Development Company located in Sugar Land, TX. He also serves as Professor and Interim Director of the Community Development Master's Program at Prairie View A & M University located within the School of Architecture. Kevin is the author of two books 40 Acres and a Mule: The African American Guide to Building Wealth Through Real Estate and Confessions of a Top Producer: Tools for Sales Success and Abundance. The Real Estate of Life is the weekly podcast Kevin host on iTunes and Google play where he talks real estate, motivation, success and life!

Kevin began his professional career as a systems analyst with ExxonMobil. His vast array of business experience, coupled with his strong entrepreneurial desires, lead him to form his own real estate company in October 2000 with a focus on helping to provide real estate brokerage services to the Greater Houston Area. In early 2005, Kevin was named the Broad Listing Broker for HUD foreclosures in the Greater Houston Area. With this contract, he had the responsibility of listing HUD Foreclosures in an 18 County area. He went on to sell more than 3,500 homes from 2007-2010. In June 2007 his real estate company was named the 22nd largest Residential Real Estate Brokerage in Houston and subsequently was named the 21st and 23rd in 2008 and 2009 by the Houston Business Journal. His TourHoustonForeclosures.com Bus Tours have been featured locally by CBS Channel 11, ABC Channel 13, Fox Channel 26 and CW Channel 39. TLC's Reality Show "Deals on the Bus" featured his foreclosure tours in March of 2009. In 2008 Kevin made the business decision to move the focus of his company toward Commercial Real Estate. He was motivated by the complexities of the transaction and the fact that Only 1% of 1% of Commercial Real Estate brokers are African American. His goal is to change that statistic!

A highly sought-after motivational speaker, he has motivated people on his views of success to corporations and organizations such as ExxonMobil, INROADS Houston, Fort Bend Independent School District, CAN Academy, and many others. Kevin's *"Tools for Success"* book has inspired countless adults and youth to reach for a higher purpose. In 2017, Kevin received from the John Maxwell Leadership Team his Certification to deliver world renown John Maxwell Leadership teachings.

Kevin is a 1991 graduate of Willowridge High School and a 2007 Wall of Honor Inductee. This Houston native received a Bachelor of Science in Computer Science with cum laude honors from Morehouse College in 1995.

Kevin attended Morehouse College on a full $75,000 Ronald E. McNair NASA Scholarship due to his academic accomplishments at Willowridge High School in Houston, Texas. With its tradition of producing leaders, Morehouse helped Kevin tap his leadership potential. He went on to hold leadership positions in a variety of campus organizations. As a further testament to Kevin's academic achievements, he received his Masters of Business Administration in Finance from the University of St. Thomas in July 2000.

Kevin's mission is to impact the lives of people socially, economically, and spiritually. With the help of God, his supportive business partner/wife, Cher, and daughter Madison, Kevin will realize his mission. He is a proud member of the Alpha Phi Alpha Fraternity, Inc., Brentwood Baptist Church, the Fort Bend Chamber of Commerce and the Greater Houston Black Chamber of Commerce.

For More Information about Kevin log on to www.KevinRiles.com

CHAPTER X

Passages
By Mark H. Tekamp

SPRING

*"My contact with the nature of God has made
me realize what I can do for God. Service is the
outcome of what is fitted to my nature. God's
call is fitted to His nature, and I never hear His
call until I have received His nature, then His
nature and mine work together, the Son of God
reveals Himself in me, and I, in my natural
life, serve the Son of God in ordinary ways,
out of…devotion to Him."*

— Oswald Chambers, *"So Send I You"*,

When did you first know that God was real? I recall myself as a
small boy of five years of age. I was standing on the part of our

black top driveway that was closest to our garage at our home in Marion, Ohio. It was a sunny day and I was standing there involved in the doing of not much of anything. Perhaps the thoughts were unusual for a boy of that age, but I remember experiencing the reality of perfection; that perfection could not only be experienced but that if sought it could be found. I wasn't sufficiently mature then to view it as a revelation from God, but since that time it has served as a sort of talisman drawing me through my years.

As I look back upon my life, I've become more aware of how much history intrudes upon our lives, even a country such as our own, which is sheltered more than most from the tragedies that occupy the story of so much of the story of human life in this world. In the early 1970's our nation's life was profoundly affected by OPEC; dramatically higher oil prices, double-digit inflation and economic recession. With the downturn in the steel industry my father, an electrical engineer, lost his job. During family dinners my father had shared with us his distress at having had to terminate the employment of increasing numbers of his subordinates. Then one day it was his turn. My father lost his job in Columbus, Ohio and found new employment in Roanoke, Virginia. Life is strange. My father loses his job. That is the reason why I have a wife named Margie and four children named Katherine, Austin, Alec and Zach and why this story that I'm sharing is the one that I have to share.

Passages

It is 1976. After a two- and one-half year absence from college, I'm resuming my education at a new school, Virginia Tech. Most of the two years I've been there, I've been in a relationship with a young lady named Carolyn. She is the most religious person I've ever known though her faith hasn't become mine. Our differences are ultimately too great to reconcile and after yet another of my threats to terminate our relationship, Carolyn accepts an offer that I didn't intend to be accepted and we're done. Two weeks later I'm conducting part of my fraternity's weekly Sunday night meeting. The stress of what I'm attempting to manage, combined with my wounded heart, leads to my beginning to hyperventilate but I succeed in regaining control of my breathing and I'm able to conclude my portion of the meeting with my audience not being aware of my condition. Two hours later, while in the bedroom of my apartment sitting at my desk busily organizing some paper relating to my fraternity's membership recruitment program, IT happened. IT wasn't either gradual or subtle. It was as though every fiber of my being had been flushed clean and been replaced with perfect love and understanding. It was as though I had stepped outside myself and saw my life exactly as I had been living it with all of its flaws exposed and all the slights I had inflicted upon my fellow man revealed. Perfect love. Perfect understanding. Completeness. Wholeness. Being a part of something that is everything. IT took me to my knees and I wept as I prayed to God that I never lose what I had just been given. IT was God's allowing me to

169

experience Heaven as well as the reality of judgment. I called Carolyn. She wept too, telling me that nothing like that had ever happened to her. It took me five years, but I came to understand the source of Carolyn's tears. God had brought Carolyn into my life. When His purpose had been served He took her away. The entire time Carolyn and I had been seeing one another she had prayed for me. When I had called, what she had heard was that her prayers had been answered.

SUMMER

"What I do for a living has offered many insights into how people go about the business of the living of their lives...One lesson I have learned that speaks most loudly to me is the power of family...When we love one another as we should we teach others not only how to love but how to be loved...Love transcends time and distance for it is the realm in which God lives."
My letter to Margie, December 24, 2012

It is May of 1982. I'm married to the daughter of a socially prominent family in Norfolk, Virginia. We, Sarah and I, were both in need of something that neither of us could give to the other. I was personally ambitious for fortune and fame and being a member of my wife's family had made me, or so I believed, important. I've been hired by Merrill Lynch and I'm feeling entirely confident that my future has been embossed in gold. I become friends with a young fellow of my age named Peter who was hired just a month or so prior to myself. We'll hear more about him later. The 1980's were long before the time of caller ID. Imagine being able to call anyone you wished to and having them actually answer the phone! So long as one was willing to work hard and swallow mega dosages of rejection along the way it was possible to build a practice capable of preserving one's employment as well as offering the ability to provide for one's family. I'm also my father in law's broker so while starting at the bottom; I also have a grasp of the golden ring at the top.

The year's pass by; Sarah and I become the parents of a daughter and a son and we're a model family, though, I'm not very successful at serving as my wife's husband. I do though love Sarah's family. My father in law and I are very close. We have the financial markets, politics and double bourbon old fashions in common. Family life may well have been ideal if it weren't for the absence of love in Sarah's and my relationship. The seeds planted in the life I lived during those years have created a revolution in what I have come to understand as being valuable. Wealth does not create meaning and purpose. Those are the gifts that flow from the sharing of our lives with others.

I leave Merrill Lynch in 1986 and transfer my practice to Prudential Securities. These are the *"yuppy"* days and yes; one of the broker's in the office really did have a poster in his office of a BMW with the tag line *"He who dies with the most toys wins."* October 1987 and the stock market crash temporarily interrupts the flow of the good times. Time though heals all wounds and the market crash becomes a profoundly impactful event without lasting consequences. My employer though enters into some hard times as the firm's embracing the allure of limited partnerships applies a serious dose of tarnish to its reputation. Many of my fellow brokers took large bites of the apple that would be the source of their fall but fortunately I held onto the tree of the financial markets as the source of my professional life.

It's 1990 and I'm now working at Paine Webber. My career is in full bloom and if a brokerage office were a football team this would have been the one I would have wanted to place a wager on. The corporate culture was squeaky clean and some of my former colleagues from prior employers found their way to the same office address. It felt like the beginning of something very good and some of it would be, but it was also the end of the life with which I was familiar with though not satisfying. Sarah and I never argued because neither of us had sufficient emotion invested in our relationship to make it worth the effort. My daughter, Katherine, was a little girl of five and my son, Austin, had only recently been born but with little keeping us together, but our children life's, centrifugal forces pulled us apart. In 1992, I chose to end my marriage, and while I'll forever regret the pain it caused those whom I love, I've always viewed it as the realization of the inevitable.

Divorce is always traumatic but mine was perhaps traumatic in a different way. I've counseled others over the years that if they were ever in love with their spouse that love can be recaptured. I believe that in the great majority of instances divorce is the worst solution to a problem. In Sarah's and my situation though, it was the recognition of what we'd never had. What I did lose though was nearly the entirety of my self-identity. I was no longer a member of her family. I lost much of what I had viewed as my social prestige; my ability to achieve my political ambitions and a future with the promise of inheriting substantial wealth. I had been the up and rising higher thirty-eight-year-old driving a seven series BMW wearing hand made suits and shirts. That person would no longer live.

Margie, the woman who would become my life, had been a broker at Prudential and I had recruited her to come to work at Paine Webber. We had our own separate practices though I helped her with hers. Our early years were years of social hibernation. We worked, and we went home. Divorce is common, but our society frowns upon the breaking up of family's and it's good that it does but recognizing that at that time there were others for whom our relationship was painful we kept a very low profile. Our non-work lives were fully occupied with one another and Margie's becoming a second mother to Katherine and Austin. Those were wonderful and romantic days and the love my children had for Margie a great source of joy for me.

In 1995, Margie and I move our practices to Smith Barney. Our new firm was an exciting place. My business was in full bloom and I was to inhabit the corner office, a visible sign of where I stood in the hierarchy of my fellow brokers. Our office was one of the most successful brokerage offices in our region and I was one of the most successful brokers in that office. Socially, I continued to live well under the radar screen but professionally I was at the top of my game.

Margie had told me of her longing to be a mother. Wishing to be supportive of all her dreams I didn't discourage the idea, though, I did counsel her that God had already blessed her with the lives of two children who deeply loved her. I thought that occasional trips to Europe for long weekends would provide some solace. We had moved to the home that we continue to live in in the Ghent area of Norfolk and as far as I was concerned our lives were full. But God and Margie had other ideas. In 1996 Margie became pregnant with our twin sons and I was to discover how, in hindsight, a life that was seemingly full would have offered so much less of the fulfillment we've received by the life that we've lived with the lives that we've been given.

FALL

"As the author of the entirety of creation all people are God's people. In His wisdom God brings His people into His world incomplete but with an innate desire to be drawn to Him in a quest for completeness. The economic, emotional and spiritual deficits of our world are not due to a lack of God's provision but rather a lack of God in His people. We stuff ourselves with the things of this world seeking to satisfy what we are lacking forgetting that God has given us spiritual eyes so that we are not reduced to seeing things as they are but that we are able to see God in all things."

My commentary on Romans 12:13

The event I'm least able to imagine is that a woman who has spent decades wishing to have children would fail to spend every possible moment experiencing the breadth and depth of every day with her children as they pass through the years of their childhood. Shortly before the birth of our twin sons, Alec and Zach, in January 1997 Margie left the work force and the life I had once lived had turned half circle; a life once lived mostly for self-had become a life focused upon others.

Charles, a recently retired Navy helicopter pilot, was a recently hired trainee. Some love technology for what technology does but there are some, and this would include Charles, love technology for what it is. The internet had recently been birthed and even during my PaineWebber days I'd become aware of the power of the computer and its great capacity to contribute to a broker's ability to manage their business. I had the assets and the ability to create significant revenue, so Charles's and my professional marriage soon followed Margie's departure. The program, which we utilized, Broker's Helper, was like magic. Our ability to closely monitor the rates of return of the individual investments of a client's portfolio gave us, we believed, the ability to enhance our client's portfolio returns.

Our office manager would receive reports detailing the volume of transactions by account and broker for the purpose of protecting the broker and the firm from accusations by the client of "*churning*", the execution of transactions for the sole purpose of creating revenue for the broker. With our recently discovered ability to manage client portfolios we would reallocate a portion of the funds that were exposed to underperforming areas of the market to those creating higher returns. Often the transactions would not generate sales commissions, but they nonetheless appeared on the reports as transactional activity. My manager at the time, Rodney, was sympathetic to what we were doing for our clients, but it was evident that he was receiving increasing pressure from his superiors to lower the volume of transactions. The day came when Rodney told me that our portfolio management strategy would have to cease. For the very first time in my now twenty year career I felt that my employer's interests were being pursued at the expense of the interests of my clients and by late 2004 Charles and I were working on our exit strategy.

Brokerage firms generate significant profits through their investment banking activity. A fiduciary standard requires the advisor without exception to place the client's interests ahead of the interests of the advisor or their employer. If brokerage firms were to permit their brokers to be held to a fiduciary standard, they would be prohibited from selling to their customers the securities that their firms are *"manufacturing"*. Making the situation still more interesting federal securities law requires that those offering investment advice must be held to a fiduciary standard. Brokerage firms claim that their brokers are not in the business of offering investment advice but rather providing information *"incidental"* to their execution of securities transactions allowing brokers to be held to a *"suitability"* standard which requires only that the broker's recommendations are *"suitable"* for their clients. Remarkably our employer had prohibited us from actively managing our client's portfolios because it revealed that we were offering our client's investment advice which our client's assumed was our responsibility but which our employer denied they were offering.

Mark H. Tekamp

In May 2004, Heritage Wealth Management Group was birthed as an independent brokerage firm affiliated with Wachovia Financial Network "*FiNet*". With half a dozen or so employees we were well staffed, but the reality was that the regulatory environment we had sought to leave behind continued to be the reality of our corporate existence since the regulations which were the bane of our professional existence were not specific to the firm but to the industry which we were still very much a part of. We had built a business prepared to deliver a level of service we were unable to provide so in less than a year we were a business needing to find a new direction.

I'll always remember that early Monday morning in April 2006. I was lying face down on the carpet in my office crying out in my spirit to God. I told God that perhaps I'd been guilty of trying to force Him to bless a business He didn't necessarily want me to be in. Possibly, He wanted me somewhere else doing something different than what I was. God wasn't angry with me, but He was very firm. "*You are where I wish you to be*" He told me. "*You have challenges, but you have received many blessings from me. Keep walking and I will walk with you.*". My response, which I believe God did not view as an impertinence was, "*All right God. Obviously, I don't know what I'm doing with this business so I'm giving it to you. Do with it as you will.*"

It's in July several months later and I'm reading an issue of "*Research Magazine*". My eyes alight upon an article titled "*On a Wing and a Prayer*" telling the story of a financial advisor named

Bryan who had surrendered his practice to God and had since been blessed by his act of surrender. I asked my friend and colleague Gary to call Bryan's office. Bryan picked right up; Gary handed the phone to me and so began Heritage's next great adventure.

I've come to realize that one can be godly without one's actions always being good. I've never doubted that Bryan is a Godly man but I'm less certain of how good he was. Human beings can be deluded, and deluded people can sometimes believe that they are following God to places that He isn't leading them to. Still, while not ignoring the pain our relationship was to cause, these were the days that my faith, like the article about Bryan, grew the wings of an eagle. I soared and flew and experienced more of God than I'd ever known existed. The vision that Bryan shared with me of building a financial advisory practice capable of transforming the financial services industry completely captured me. Bryan, while bringing me closer to God, also delivered Heritage from the brokerage industry to the advisory world, the world where the fiduciary standard serves as the coin of the realm. In January 2007 Heritage merged with Bryan's advisory practice and together we became "*Highway Financial Networks*".

In one of Bryan's and my first conversations, he had uttered words, which caused my heart to dance. "*Capital will not be a problem.*" As subsequent events were to reveal truer words have been spoken. A caution sign that I may well have been able to see had I been looking for it was the trail of broken relationships that Bryan had experienced throughout his professional life. He felt himself at times to have been betrayed or abandoned by those whom he had counted upon to follow him. He was though fairly well connected, and he had friends in high places though few had been sufficiently friendly to write him checks. Heritage's cash flow was paying the bills for the business and the cash flow wasn't sufficient to cover our current expenses as well as providing seed capital to support the rolling out of Highway as a multi office national advisory practice. I recall the conversation at a restaurant with Bryan and another colleague, Don, when I first became aware of how dire our financial situation was. Not many days later I was deep in prayer when I felt the Lord had placed a name before me as our "*capital investor*". I was excited to share the name with Bryan and it was a joyous day for us when Bryan flew to Norfolk and our prospective capital investor became our capital investor in fact.

The second half of 2007 was a truly exciting time. Bryan's vision, wedded to capital, was more than capable of attracting a retinue of talented followers and the advisory practice that was being birthed would be born wearing the best of swaddling clothes. Our corporate reach though exceeded our grasp and by the time we entered 2008 we began to miss payroll. At our office in Norfolk on Wednesday mornings at 7 am a group of us would gather in our first floor conference room for our weekly Bible study and prayer. I wonder if my father came to rue the existence of that day in the week for it would be on that day that I would call my father to ask for money. My father never said no but he was never happy with the hearing of my request and the words I offered him which I really did believe about our future times of bounty were words I'm certain he'd long since ceased to believe. I remember thinking to myself that if I'd had a choice between severing my little finger and having to ask my father for money, I'd gladly have surrendered the finger if only it could have paid the mortgage.

By the summer of 2008 I ceased to be the last of Bryan's followers. I'd been the most loyal and had been willing to make significant personal sacrifices to keep the dream alive but allowing our ability to serve our client's to be put at risk was a price I was not willing to pay. I remember my phone call to Bryan when I told him that the time had come to separate our practices. We would be willing to support him with some portion of our revenue, but the time had come to realize that God was not blessing what he had sought to build. Bryan was not happy, but we had not lost our ability to work with one another. He told me he would call me back within several days with an estimate of what share of the overall revenue he would require. In early to mid-July all went according to plan with Norfolk hobbled but not on its knees. On the Tuesday following the Labor Day holiday I returned to my office to discover that I'd received a phone message from Bryan alluding to our need to discuss the mid October revenue allocation. I returned the phone call with some trepidation and Bryan told me that there would be little to no revenue to share with Norfolk. I told Bryan that we'd had an agreement and that our agreement was non-negotiable. The phone call ended and with it my ability to trust one whom I'd grown to view as my brother.

Within several weeks both Charles and I received termination notices stating that we were no longer employees of Highway. To add more spice to the mix, Bryan had filed a complaint with the Virginia State Corporation Commission alleging impropriety on Charles's and my part with a specific reference to our '*theft*' of corporate data. What followed were Charles's finest days during all the years of our relationship. Bryan's intent was to gain possession of our advisory relationships, collect the entirety of the revenue they generated and leave Charles and I pondering alternative opportunities for employment. Charles responded by having our clients sign letters terminating their advisory relationship with Highway with the result being that Bryan had lost his ability to capture revenue from our client relationships.

It would take five months but on Tuesday, February 24, 2009 colleague, friend and fellow parishioner of St. Paul's Episcopal Church, Gary, walked up to Margie and I who were seated at a table having our church's Shrove Tuesday dinner and gave us the wonderful news that the state corporation commission had approved the "*rebirth*" of Heritage Wealth Management Group version 2.0. We had regained our capacity to have our client's pay us for our work.

2008 was the year of the Global Financial Crisis with the unfortunate consequence that our clients had at least temporarily lost 25% of the value of their assets and Heritage an equal amount of its revenue. Another casualty of the financial crisis was our landlord who had taken on significant debt to construct some apartments, which were sitting empty. The bank foreclosed on our landlord and Heritage now found itself to be a business without a home. For six months Charles managed the building out of our new office space conveniently located within five minutes walking distance from my home from which I would be working during that time.

The wheels of time keep turning and we're now at 2012. On a Sunday evening in April, while seated in our den watching television, I began to experience strange palpitations in my abdominal cavity, which became increasingly uncomfortable. Near midnight I tell Margie that I need to go to the hospital and so begins my journey with Stage 3 Level IV Colon Cancer; a diagnosis most of those who receive it do not survive. My intent is not to veer off here into an extended discourse upon my dance with cancer, but this is a dance that should change how one looks at life and it certainly changed mine. What I'd like to share of that experience I believe is best described by a brief excerpt from a talk I'd delivered in 2017 while serving in Kairos prison ministry.

> *"I stand before you today not being able to lay a claim to any extraordinary personal qualities. I'm not a hero and I'm often a fool. But when I started out on that journey, I did do one thing, which completely revolutionized the nature of my journey with cancer. I gave it to God. I*

asked Him to use my cancer as His means of revealing Himself to those who would share this journey with me; family, friends, members of the health care profession. I asked Him to use me to show others how to live and, if it was His will, how to die.

During the year when my health dominated my life, I experienced many things but I never experienced fear. I was in God's hands and He would deliver me. I didn't need to know where but only that He would.

And God did answer my prayers. There were aspects of my journey that were miraculous. God did reveal Himself to others through my illness. He did use my illness as His means of healing others. And He used my illness to heal me."

It is those final few sentences that particularly resonate with me. Post cancer, I've acquired a passionate desire for healing and a dramatically enhanced capacity to sense the brokenness not just of the physical sort but more often of the emotional that inhabits so many including those whom I serve in my role of financial advisor.

It is as though I've been given the gift of reaching into the heart of another and making their pain as well as their pleasure my own. It is now much easier for me to shed tears and I have a significantly enhanced ability to experience the joy of life and I've learned that they aren't opposites but rather different expressions of the same thing.

The Registered Investment Advisory (RIA) business of which Heritage is a part is a descendent of the financial planning profession. The core of the advisor client relationship is the identification of the client's financial goals with the investments cast in the role as the means of the achieving of those goals. Having money without a purpose is like a journey without a destination. The most beautiful part of financial planning is that it brings the advisor and the client together in seeking to accomplish what the client cares most about; their ability to provide for those whom they love. While the advisory business does this pretty well, much of the remainder of the financial services industry does not. Fear and greed are spiritual qualities that often characterize people's attitudes towards their wealth. This is a form of spiritual "*virus*" which not only investors are subject to but those whom they rely upon for financial advice. When clients discover that they have sufficient resources to achieve their financial goals they are set free. Money becomes a servant rather than a master and it becomes a means of the dispensing of blessing for others.

Over the course of 2013 my journey with cancer begins to fade into my life's background and I resume my previous level of involvement in this business. While I've been away though, physically and emotionally, the business has changed. When Heritage was reconstituted, Charles was given the title of President with his focusing upon the managing of the administrative parts of the business while my responsibility was client relationship management. Charles has grown in his role and become increasingly motivated by his own passions and interests, which don't necessarily coincide with what I view as the primary purpose of being a financial advisory practice. Increasingly he manages the various details of the business including its finances by relying solely upon his own counsel. William has joined our business as our financial planning person and Gary is still present if not being fully utilized. Alec and Zach are on the cusp on entering college, so Margie now has more time to act as my client services support individual. Bob has also joined us as our second full time advisor. The revenue I'm responsible for generating is supporting almost the entirety of the business with the result that I'm being compensated at a level of approximately half of what most advisors earn with my level of revenue generation, resulting in Margie's and my continuing to experience financial challenges.

In the summer of 2013, my father, who has supported my family through our lean years with Bryan, moves into our home. He is diagnosed with late stage Alzheimer's and though he is a shadow of the man he was we are able to use our home as his home and in his final months we are able to offer him what he is left with the ability to value; our love and ability to comfort him. It is a revelation of the symmetry of love that our house has become his home because it was his generosity that allowed us to keep our home. In February 2014 I find my father in his bed on the 3rd floor of our home but he has left us. He is gone but he continues to provide for us as I am his heir.

2015 arrives and with its Margie and I enter into a season of death as I have five clients pass on in the year's first two months. Interestingly, I have the opportunity in several instances to serve as executor of their estates allowing me to create additional income for my family. We never have too much, but most often we have just enough.

Our son's Alec and Zach graduate from high school in June of that year and it was during that summer that I had one of my favorite experiences with God. I had walked to Fleet Park where my sons had once played Little League baseball. It was a picture-perfect day, a Sunday near the noon hour. As I reach the place where I turn around and head back for home I'm standing next to the railroad tracks and as I look across them I see a plastic trash bag levitating perhaps six feet above the ground supported by a cone shaped pocket of air given visible form by the sand and gravel that it had drawn upwards while supporting the plastic bag. I was tempted to take a picture, but I chose not to for I knew it was mine alone to see and I knew who it was that wanted me to see it. As I walk nearly a mile I stand by another set of railroad tracks and I observe exactly the same thing one more time. Over the next several mornings, I try to interpret during my time of prayer what

God was trying to tell me. It may have been the third morning following that I finally got it. I have two sons. The railroad tracks were symbolic of my son's leaving their home. The levitating trash bags were God's way of telling me that His spirit would be going with them.

2016 dawns and Charles & Gary offer me the opportunity I'd long been seeking; the ability to create additional income to provide for my family by growing my business. The plan is detailed and for several months I enthusiastically embrace the ability to ensure my family's financial well-being. It may have been near July when the Lord told me to back off and to work on my relationship with Him rather than pursuing my financial security. I heard God's voice clearly and He was telling me *"You are seeking to have Me follow you, but it is you who I want to follow Me."* I worked forty hours a week and I took care of those I was responsible for but I'm both glad and relieved to be able to say I was obedient. I dramatically increased my time in prayer and began to substitute Christian novels for the works of history I've long favored. I'd been walking for years with the Lord. I'd create documents on my cell phone and pause to memorize passages along the way. I learned why the words of The Bible are described as the living word. My life became *"all God all the time"* and He and I were seldom apart from one another. Gary and Charles would subsequently criticize me for my changed behavior but being obedient to God isn't something I felt the need to apologize for.

2017 arrives and God tells me that it's time for graduation and its time for me to work both long hours and with great diligence. He tells me that he'll bless my efforts and that the results of my work will be revelations of His glory. The year really is amazing. I encountered new relationships and grew the dollar value of the assets I'm responsible for at a rate I'd never experienced since the first several years of my career. My efforts create an additional $100,000 in revenue for our business. Something strange though is happening in the relationship between Charles and me.

Charles's skills at time management would often leave me frustrated though I'd never lost my admiration for his mastery of technology. The reality, though, is that the two of us had lost our ability to work with one another. Often, I would seek his assistance in the performing of specific tasks but his delay in responding would leave me angry. Eventually I traded anger for resignation and I stopped asking for his help except in those few instances when an alternative wasn't available. Charles has, though, grown passionate about his involvement in the field of electronic media; both book publishing and pod casting.

We'd had a meeting with Jeffrey, a friend and a management consultant, regarding our business. He had asked us collectively to describe what the purpose of our business was but to respond individually. I thought the answer was obvious. Heritage Wealth Management Group is a financial advisory practice. It pays our bills. It's what we do. Charles would not agree to that definition. He suggested that our corporate purpose was still being defined and not yet apparent.

God and I spent many hours pondering over a quandary that had become a gordian knot. Charles is a professed believer. I knew that God had plans to grow our business as well as to bless those whom He chose to be part of it. Charles and I had visions that were not only different but in competition with one another. The dramatic growth of our revenue in 2017, though, had given me what I believed to be another talisman. I would approach William and Gary and ask if they felt that it should be our businesses primary objective to identify and pursue opportunities for growth. They agreed. The taste of success was seductive which I'm certain explains 2016 and my time with God and 2017 and the revelation of His blessings. How though to cut that Gordian knot of having Charles seeking to go one-way and my seeking to go another? I came to believe that for God's vision for Heritage to be realized that Charles would need to be separated from us; but how? Charles had sole oversight of our finances. He had sole control over our various platforms, which allow us to serve our clients. Charles had burrowed very deeply into the blood stream of the business and had he believed made himself indispensable to it.

Something I always have and will believe is that God had given Bryan a vision as to how he was to be used to transform the financial services industry. The integrity of that vision is something I'm willing to believe without the slightest reservation. When Bryan's pursuit of that vision failed, I don't believe it was a failure of God's vision but rather of Bryan's ability to achieve it. I also believe that that vision was meant to be transplanted to this business and that it will be this business that will lead to its fulfillment. I acknowledge the boldness of this claim but I know that God is capable of achieving it. The miracles described in these pages I believe are proof of this.

2018 arrives and with its God's pronouncement to me that He is preparing to lead us to the land of His promise. I couldn't see how but that wasn't my responsibility, so I settled for knowing that it would happen. Late the prior year, I'd driven to old friend Peter's home (he of my Merrill Lynch training days in 1982) three hours away. He had recently retired and had become a client. I'd felt God telling me that Peter was the one to lead the business and I described to him the opportunity that I felt would be his if he chose to accept it. He never wavered and though our way forward was significantly less than clear, we knew that we had a destiny to share with one another. In the following months, I would mention Peter's name to William and Gary and Margie. My wife would look at me through fish eyes expressing her bewilderment that something that made so much sense to me would for her be so incomprehensible. Our leader had been revealed but not yet his opportunity to lead.

I did not know it then, but at the same time Peter and I were having our conversations, Gary and Charles were discussing Heritage's need to improve the management of its finances. Gary had grown close to an individual named Steve and with all the

God stories contained within these pages this is one of the very best. Steve walks more closely with God than almost anyone I've ever known, and I flatter myself in believing that I'm able to see God at work in his life the way I believe He is at work in mine. Steve is also an accountant operating with a very high level of intellect who also had a significant amount of time available and a wish to generate additional income. As God gave us Peter, so, He also gave us Steve. Only Steve could have done the work that he needed to do and only Steve had the additional relationships that allowed us to be delivered to the ground that we've been given to occupy. Steve began his work in March of 2018 and month by month the iceberg that served as a metaphor of our corporate life was raised up and much that had for so long been hidden was now exposed to the antiseptic quality of light.

As the months progressed it became evident that Charles's time with us was coming to its end. Gary and I would have conversations about the prospective date of Charles's separation, but the month kept slipping backwards. July became September then October and now it was November. Gary had sought the services of an attorney to make certain all details were being properly managed and that the necessary documents to effectuate Charles's separation were in order.

Just before November 20, 2018 and Charles, Steve, Gary and I meet in one of our office's conference rooms. It has been made clear to me that Charles is now prepared to sign his separation agreement. The atmosphere in the room is more warm than cool without any evidence of anger or hint of tempers set to explode. Steve starts the conversation and Gary follows. Charles responds, and it becomes apparent that Charles is not only not prepared to resign but appears to have not even given it serious consideration. He admits that mistakes have been made but that we are now able to move forwards and that he should continue to occupy the position of President. In this bit of drama, I do not wish to cast myself in the role of hero, but I did feel that I had a role to play and a card to put on the table. *"Charles"*, I said, *"you cannot continue to lead when there isn't anyone willing to follow you."* The words were so obviously true they couldn't be argued with. Charles acknowledged their truth and he agreed to the terms of his separation.

This is being written just over five months later. Peter is on board as Chief Operating Officer. He has earned the respect as well as the affection of all his colleagues and if he were to change his name to how others view how he is fulfilling his role it would be *"awesome"*. Margie has remarked how for so many months she was left to wonder what if any role he would ever have to play in our business but now she describes how he is fulfilling the role he is playing as *"perfect"*.

Gary has become the man of iron he has always been. Our friendship of twenty years has been rebirthed and there is a kindness and gentleness in our repartee that had long been absent. In our earliest months since Charles's separation he was, if not always, the first to arrive (I'm a keeper of notoriously early hours) always the last to leave. He has been blessed financially by the business as he has been a blessing to it and so like my father and our home it's another revelation of the symmetry of love.

Steve has been described previously but I would wish to add that he too is destined to play a vital role in the future well being of this business. God knew His name before we knew it and who he is and what he will do is what was always meant to be. Steve exhausts the list of terms one can use to describe a personality. His is a life lived in vivid colors and he can teach a child how to laugh.

Margie's and my life together has been a continuous source of joy for me, but it is a life that has been transformed. For so many years my wife has labored under the cross of our financial challenges with her seeking to shelter me from issues not related to my role as relationship manager for those whom this business serves. With the financial restructuring of our business, for the first time since the beginning of our relationship, we've experienced the peace of financial security. The price we've paid, though, to arrive where we are, has been small in relation to the benefits of what we've received; a greatly enhanced capacity to comprehend the reality of God and how extraordinary His presence in this world is. Here is the perfect place to share my final God story.

Three years ago, I'd received correspondence from Citigroup, which had been the owner of Smith Barney during my years of employment there. The correspondence indicated that I was entitled to the receipt of my pension benefit and, that if I so chose, I could receive a check as a lump sum payment for the amount. I made several phone calls to the firm handling Citigroup's pension management and twice received assurances that I was entitled to receive a lump sum payment. Happy to be in receipt of good news, I asked that they send me the documents. It was the summer of our son's first year of college so it would have been 2016. Alec and I had spent an enjoyable several hours on a harbor tour boat cruise and I return home to see the Citigroup pension envelope. I open it and read the documents but don't see any reference to my receiving a lump sum payment. I make a phone call and find out that only employees with ten years of employment qualify to receive a lump payment and I don't qualify.

Fast forward to January of this year. I receive another envelope from Citigroup. I'm eligible to receive my pension and guess what? The lump sum option is back. I call once. I call twice. I call a third time. Yes, is yes is yes. On a Friday evening, I walk downstairs to visit with Margie who is watching television. God has placed a thought upon my heart and He wants me to share it with her. I tell her that with our being due to receive the check in early April, we'll have the funds in time to give each of our sons a generous present next month upon their graduation from college. Margie cries. Remember the story of the levitating trash bags?

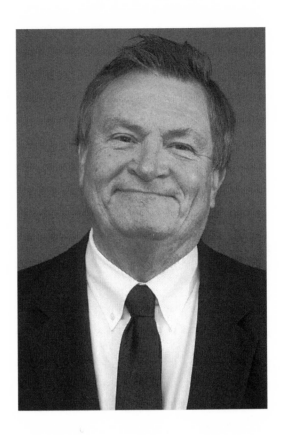

Mark H Tekamp | Bio

Mark was born in 1954 the son of a World War Two veteran and a mother who may have worn pearls while pushing a vacuum cleaner like Donna Reed. Growing up in Ohio his family moved to Roanoke, Virginia in 1974 and graduated from Virginia Tech with a Bachelors Degree in Business Administration in 1978. While working in the college publishing industry in New Orleans he received a MBA from the University of New Orleans in 1982.

In 1982 Mark moved to Norfolk, Virginia to pursue employment in the financial services industry working as a broker for a number of national firms including Merrill Lynch and Smith Barney. In 2004 Mark and several colleagues established Heritage Wealth Management Group, a Registered Investment Advisor (RIA) practice where he continues to be employed as Financial Advisor, Chief Investment Strategist and owner.

The father of four and the husband of Margie Mark pursues an active interest in the financial markets, history and seeking a deeper understanding of what God seeks to reveal to us through His word. Active in Kairo prison ministry he also is an active walker often while listening to audio books. He counts his listening to the entirety of Shelby Foote's 2,986 page civil war trilogy which took 616 miles as one of his more notable accomplishments.

CHAPTER XI

How Does Success Work As A Christian In A Secular Business World?

By Scott McGregor

"Winning isn't everything; it's the only thing"

— UCLA Bruins Football Coach Henry Russell "Red" Sanders

Q. What is the chief end of man?
A. Man's chief end is to glorify God,
and to enjoy Him forever.

WESTMINSTER SHORTER CATECHISM

How do we reconcile these two viewpoints? What is success? If I make a bunch of money, acquire a bunch of things and show the world my material success, what does that mean?

How do I show my faith through my actions in the marketplace? Does God want successful businessmen? What if my business, or career, is not as successful as I would like? What do I do with that?

So many questions. ...

I believe that God wants us to be successful. Why would He not want people to succeed and to have a positive impact on the world to reflect His Glory? The ultimate question is what does it mean to be successful? Is it power? Is it the size of our investment portfolio? Where does integrity fit in? Is it true that Malcolm Forbes was right when he said, *"He who dies with the most toys wins."*?

As I examine these questions with you, it occurs to me that it might be helpful to give you some background on myself and my walk-through life with, and at times without, The Lord.

I was born in the 60's. As a baby boomer my world was textbook from the days of the 50's. Your path was pretty much set for you. You went to school, got good grades, got a college degree, got married, had kids, attended church, succeeded at work, were a pillar in the community and a nice guy to boot. That is the way it was done. So, I did all those things. And I was good at it. I had some stumbles along the way, but by the world's measures I did pretty well. I joined a big company, which was a secular, but moral, entity and rose through the ranks over time into a position where I

How Does Success Work As A Christian In A Secular Business World?

was responsible for a business unit and in the top 100 positions of a Fortune 300 company with about 30,000 employees.

Paralleling this business stuff was my spiritual growth. I came to know The Lord Jesus Christ in my teens. As a reformed believer, I hold to the view of *"once saved, always saved"*, while at the same time believing that faith without works is dead. What that meant in my life is that I had to be rescued many times from the foibles of youth before I got it through my thick skull that to live without Jesus Christ as Lord and Savior is a path to destruction. Once I finally figured that out, I found opportunities to increasingly reflect Him in my daily efforts.

One of my many flaws is the viewpoint that if you just work harder than anyone else you will persevere. While I continue to believe in making a strong effort in anything you do, to arrogantly assume that the success is solely in your hands is ridiculous. It is a trap, an evil trap that can lead to isolation, desolation and misery. In addition to my *"work myself to death"* approach to success I combined that with an unhealthy dose of perfectionism, so much so that I could not enjoy any success, no matter how great, without worrying about how I could have done it better. What a mess!

So where is my faith in all of this? During most of my business career I was also in positions of leadership in my church. I served with intensity and was committed to making those churches better. I will let you in on a little thing I learned about church work. No matter how much *"good"* you do, the *"why"* you are doing it is more important that the "*how*" you are doing it. I did church very well, but in many cases, it was an extension of business, make things run better cause that's what I do. That isn't a faith matter; it is not the works that lead to life. It is being a good guy willing to help, not a bad trait, but not necessarily pointed towards glorifying God.

To the world, I had it all. Loving wife, two wonderful successful children, respect and impact at church. I gave the credit to God, deflecting any personal credit in business or church success. Clearly, I was glorifying God. Or was I?

Self-examination is a very intense, emotional and potentially terrifying process. If we strip away all that the world sees, all that our family sees, all that our business and church colleagues see, we are left with the reality of how we see ourselves.

Today, I consider myself as an individual who has had both business success and spiritual success, yet with so much room to grow, particularly spiritually. I know there are people that I associate with and those that love me that would point out all that I have done and argue strongly that I have been more successful than I think I have. By the world's viewpoint it would be hard to argue that I have not been largely successful. In the end, however, we all must deal with our own view AND compare that to what we understand we are called to by our Lord.

So, why is it that I don't consider myself more of a success? It is because I haven't arrived yet at where God would have me be. We serve an ever loving, ever forgiving and indescribably generous

How Does Success Work As A Christian
In A Secular Business World?

God. My chief end is to glorify Him, and in that I am a work in process, as most likely, you are as well. I have had moments where God has been glorified, but to say that I have arrived would be a gross overstatement. This begs the question, however. . .

How do we glorify God?

First, we need to get to *know* Him. If you are a believer, we glorify God through obeying him and truly making Him Lord of your life. Too often we accept Jesus as Savior, yet don't quite fully buy into him as Lord of our lives. And yes, I am being convicted of that as I write this! You must surrender to Him, to understand His character and to behave in a way that would have Him say "*Well done good and faithful servant*". I desperately want to hear Jesus say that to me!

If you are not a believer, you need to ask yourself the question, what or who do I believe in? I have come to the conclusion that life makes absolutely no sense at all in the absence of a Sovereign God Who is perfect, who loves me more than I can imagine and sent his Son Jesus Christ to death to rescue me from my sins, those actions or inactions that were not Holy and absent of rescue would separate me from God. So, if you don't know Jesus Christ as your Lord and Savior it is impossible to fully Glorify God. That is a hard statement. It is also true. So, in my view, there is one action that must take place. Get to know about Jesus and ask him into your life.

How to Be Born Again
By Billy Graham

A man named Nicodemus came to Jesus by night. Perhaps he was afraid of criticism or he had a desire for a private conversation, or maybe he wanted to know more before committing himself to Jesus Christ. In any event, he came and asked Jesus some questions.

Jesus looked at him and said, "Nicodemus, you need to be born again" (Cf. John 3:5). In fact, He said, "Verily, verily"—and any time Jesus used that expression, He meant that what was to follow was very important. He said, "Verily, verily, I say unto thee ... ye must be born again" (John 3:5,7, KJV).

Have you been born again? Call it conversion, call it commitment, call it repentance, call it being saved, but has it happened to you? Does Christ live in your heart? Do you know it?

*Many people have thought a long time about religion and Christianity and yet have never made a commitment. **Are you committed to Jesus Christ?***

Nicodemus must have been stunned when Jesus said, "You must be born again." It wouldn't seem shocking if Christ had said that to Zacchaeus the tax collector or to the thief on the cross or to the woman caught in adultery. But Nicodemus was one of the great religious leaders of his time. Still, he was searching for reality.

*You may go to church, but perhaps you are still searching. There is an empty place in your heart, and something inside tells you that you're not really **right with God.** Nicodemus fasted two days a week. He spent two hours every day in prayer. He tithed. Why did Jesus say that Nicodemus must be born again? Because He could read the heart of Nicodemus. Jesus saw that Nicodemus had covered himself with religion but had not yet found fellowship with God.*

The Root of Our Problems

What causes all of our troubles in the world—lying and cheating and hate and prejudice and social inequality and war? Jesus said, "But those things which proceed out of the mouth come from the heart, and they defile a man" (Matthew 15:18). He said the problem is in our hearts; our hearts need to be changed.

Psychologists, sociologists and psychiatrists all recognize that there is something wrong with humankind. Many words in Scripture describe it. Among them is the word **transgression:** *"Sin is the transgression of the law" (1 John 3:4, KJV). What law? The Law of Moses, the Ten Commandments. Have you ever broken one of those Commandments? Then you are guilty of having broken them all (James 2:10).*

The word sin carries with it the idea of missing the mark, coming short of our duty, failure to do what we ought to do. The Bible says, "All unrighteousness is sin" (1 John 5:17, KJV). And yet before we can get to heaven, we must have righteousness. God says, "Be perfect as I am perfect, holy as I am holy" (Matthew 5:48, 1 Peter 1:16).

Where are we going to get that perfection? We don't have it now, yet we can't get to heaven if we don't have it. That is why Christ died on the cross; He shed His blood and rose again to provide righteousness for us.

*Another word is **iniquity**, which means to turn aside from the straight path. Isaiah said, "All we like sheep have gone astray; We have turned, every one, to his own way; And the Lord has laid on Him the iniquity of us all" (Isaiah 53:6).*

*The Bible says, "Therefore, just as through one man sin entered the world, and death through sin ... thus death spread to all men, because all sinned" (Romans 5:12). Every person needs a **radical change**. We need to have our sins forgiven; we need to be clothed in the* *righteousness of God. To find fulfillment in this life we need to find something to commit ourselves to. Are you a committed person? What are you committed to? Why don't you make Christ your cause and follow Him? He will never let you down.*

The New Birth

Some people ask the question: What is new birth? Nicodemus asked that question too: "How can a man be born when he is old?" He wanted to understand it.

I was born and reared on a dairy farm. How can a black cow eat green grass and produce white milk and yellow butter? I don't understand that. I might say, "Because I don't understand it, I'm never going to drink milk again." And you'd say, "You're crazy."

I don't understand it, but I accept it by faith. Nicodemus could see only the physical and the material, but Jesus was talking about the spiritual.

*How is the new birth accomplished? We cannot
inherit new birth. The Bible says that those
who are born again "were born, not of blood,
nor of the will of the flesh, nor of the will of
man, but of God" (John 1:13). Our fathers and
mothers may be the greatest born-again
Christians in the world, but that doesn't make
us born-again Christians, too. Many people
have the idea that because they were born into a
Christian home, they are automatically
Christians. They're not.*

*We cannot work our way to God, either. The
Bible says that salvation comes "not by works of
righteousness which we have done, but
according to His mercy He saved us, through the
washing of regeneration and renewing of the
Holy Spirit" (Titus 3:5).*

*Nor is reformation enough. We can say, "I am
going to turn over a new leaf," or "I am going to
make New Year's resolutions." But Isaiah said*

that in the sight of God "all our righteousnesses are like filthy rags" (Isaiah 64:6).

Some of us have changed on the outside to conform to certain social standards or behavior that is expected of us in our churches, but down inside we have never been changed. That is what Jesus was talking to Nicodemus about. He said, "Nicodemus, you need changing inside," and only the Holy Spirit can do that. Being born from above is a supernatural act of God. The Holy Spirit convicts us of our sin; He disturbs us because we have sinned against God. And then the Holy Spirit regenerates us. That is when we are born again. The Holy Spirit comes to live in our hearts to help us in our daily lives. The Spirit of God gives us assurance, gives us joy, produces fruit in our lives and teaches us the Scriptures.

Some people try to imitate Christ. They think that all we have to do is try to follow Jesus and try to do the things He did, and we will get into heaven. But we can't do it. We may know the

*religious songs. We may even say prayers. But if
we haven't been to the foot of the cross, we
haven't been born again. That is the message
Jesus is trying to teach us.*

*To be born again means that "[God] will give
you a new heart and put a new spirit within
you" (Ezekiel 36:26). "Old things have passed
away; behold, all things have become new" (2
Corinthians 5:17). We are "partakers of the
divine nature" (2 Peter 1:4); we have "passed
from death into life" (John 5:24). The new
birth brings about a change in our philosophy
and manner of living.*

The Mystery

*There is a mystery to the new birth. Jesus said,
"The wind blows where it wishes, and you hear
the sound of it, but cannot tell where it comes
from and where it goes" (John 3:8). But you can
see the result. Jesus did not attempt to explain
the new birth to Nicodemus; our finite minds*

cannot understand the infinite. We come by simple childlike faith, and we put our faith in Jesus Christ. When we do, we are born again.

It happens this way. First we have to hear the Word of God. "Faith comes by hearing, and hearing by the word of God" (Romans 10:17). That is the first step. "It pleased God through the foolishness of the message preached to save those who believe" (1 Corinthians 1:21). It sounds foolish that words from a Bible have the power to penetrate our hearts and change our lives, but they do, because they are God's holy words.

Then there is the work of the Holy Spirit. He convicts: "And when He has come, He will convict the world of sin, and of righteousness, and of judgment" (John 16:8). He changes us. He changes our wills, our affections, our objectives for living, our disposition. He gives us a new purpose and new goals. "Old things pass away, and everything becomes new" (Cf. 2 Corinthians 5:17). Then He indwells us: "Do

*you not know that you are the temple of God
and that the Spirit of God dwells in you?" Does
God the Holy Spirit live in you?*

*Jesus Christ says that we must be born again.
How do we become born again? By repenting of
sin. That means we are willing to change our
way of living. We say to God, "I'm a sinner,
and I'm sorry." It's simple and childlike. Then
by faith we receive Jesus Christ as our Lord and
Master and Savior. We are willing to follow
Him in a new life of obedience, in which the
Holy Spirit helps us as we read the Bible and
pray and witness.*

*If there is a doubt in your mind about whether
you have been born again, I hope you will settle
it now, because the Bible says in 2 Corinthians
6:2, "Now is the accepted time; ... [today] is the
day of salvation."*

Second,

Once we know Who we are glorifying, the question becomes, how do we know we are glorifying Him?

The alternative to glorifying God is to take full credit for what we do. If we experience success, we can certainly take pride in what we have done and acknowledge that our efforts played a role in the successful endeavor. At the same time, the question we must ask ourselves is – who shall get the credit?

Worldly success is just that, worldly. It has no lasting impact. King Solomon, perhaps the richest and wisest King in all of Israel, wrote the following about worldly success and possessions. . .

Everything Is Meaningless

Ecclesiastes 1 New International Version (NIV)

¹ The words of the Teacher, [a] son
of David, king in Jerusalem:
² "Meaningless! Meaningless!" says the Teacher.
"Utterly meaningless!
Everything is meaningless."
³ What do people gain from all their labors

at which they toil under the sun?
 ⁴ Generations come and generations go,
but the earth remains forever.
 ⁵ The sun rises and the sun sets,
and hurries back to where it rises.
 ⁶ The wind blows to the south and turns to the
north; round and round it goes,
ever returning on its course.
 ⁷ All streams flow into the sea, yet the sea is
never full. To the place the streams come from,
there they return again.
 ⁸ All things are wearisome, more than one can
say. The eye never has enough of seeing, nor
the ear its fill of hearing.
 ⁹ What has been will be again,
what has been done will be done again;
there is nothing new under the sun.
 ¹⁰ Is there anything of which one can say,
"Look! This is something new"?
It was here already, long ago;
it was here before our time.
 ¹¹ No one remembers the former generations,

and even those yet to come

will not be remembered by those

who follow them.

Contrast this text with that before of Malcolm Forbes about accumulating toys.

Who's right? Is worldly success all meaningless as Solomon suggests? The answer is YES, unless it is used to lift up the Almighty.

Here's the premise of the argument. We are loved by God. So much so that he sent his Son Jesus Christ to die to atone for our sins. We owe Him everything, so any success we might have is not a result of what our flesh created but what He created in us, so that he might be Glorified.

David Platt says it this way: The message of biblical Christianity is not *"God loves me, period."* The message of biblical Christianity is *"God loves me so that I might make Him – His ways, His salvation, His glory, and His greatness known among all nations. God is the object of our faith, and Christianity centers around him. We are not the end of the Gospel, God is."*

How do I think I might have glorified God during my business career? By being an example, a light where possible. Never forget, no matter what your position in a business, that people are watching you to see how you act, what you say and what is important. I would like to think that I was a positive influence on people, not only in a business sense, but more importantly, in a faith sense. As you approach difficult situations or joyous ones, how you handle them and how you reflect your faith in doing so, is a key to living out your faith. My career overall was very positive, but I am proudest of my behavior, my faith journey and my light, during those times when things were not going as well as the company or I might like. Be authentic, it is okay to acknowledge a failure or a shortcoming, while at the same time be particularly mindful that your witness is at its most powerful when you are not at your highest point, but when you are at your lowest. To the extent I have a legacy from my business career, it is not measured in financial or positional terms, but in the impact, I had in people's lives showing them light and some insight into a life lived in faith.

I absolutely believe that it is possible to be successful in business while living out your faith in a positive manner. If you are true to the principles of seeking the Mind of Christ in what you do you will influence people in a positive way and that will be your lasting imprint on their lives. The key is to always remember - *it is not about you. It is about Him*.

Presenting our success as His success is the only answer. Dying to self to gain for His kingdom is the way to deal with success in a way that is restorative, not destructive. While it can be much easier to present yourself as a success in a worldly way, it is like King Solomon says "*futile*". It has no lasting weight to it. Dust to the wind. It seems much easier but is much shallower. You can stay out of trouble, do good things, be a nice person, acquire stuff, give to charities, volunteer your time to the community, promote yourself and you will generally be viewed as successful in the world, but to what end. Why does it matter? It only truly matters if it serves a Kingdom purpose for the Lord God Almighty and His Son Jesus Christ.

Glorifying God is much more difficult in my experience, but oh so much more rewarding. We know that we are Glorifying God when the fruit of our efforts lifts Him up. For I would suggest that scripture is very instructive in this matter as it discusses fruits of The Spirit from God.

Galatians 5:22 gives us nine examples:

Love
Joy
Peace
Longsuffering
Kindness
Goodness
Faithfulness
Gentleness
Self-control

If you exhibit these things with great regularity you are on the right path. To challenge you further, these behaviors MUST be exhibited not only publicly, but more importantly, privately. If you are exhibiting these things publicly but not privately, I would suggest to you that you examine your heart, your motives and seek The Lord for a change in your life because to Serve Him is to give him your whole heart, not only the heart that the world sees. As a man who can rightly be accused and convicted of hypocrisy in a number of cases where fruits of the spirit are concerned, you must be honest with yourself and God about these matters. Ask Him to change your heart and HE WILL!

So, that all sounds really good but at the same time seems impossible, especially when we must engage in the workplace where these views might be foreign, or antithetical to success in business. At this point I think it might be helpful to examine the quote *"Preach the Gospel at all times, when necessary use words"*. Which has been attributed in one form or another to Francis Assisi, a 13th century Catholic Friar.

In most businesses that I am familiar with open expressions of faith are either expressly prohibited or, at a minimum, frowned upon. As a result, our opportunity to teach and lead others to Christ is limited to our actions, generally not our words.

How do you interact with those around you? Are you kind, generous, considerate? When situations arise where there are off color behaviors, rude or foul language, course teasing or belittling of others – what do you do?

How will people see a difference in you versus what the world generally has to offer? It is by your actions or inactions that people will form an impression, especially when you are not able to preach or extort others through the verbal language of your faith.

Here are some guiding principles to showing light and a Christian witness that I would like you to consider:

1. Always take the high road. I am not aware of a situation where the name of Jesus is lifted high if we choose to get down in the dirt in a difficult situation. Whether you know Jesus or not, going down the wrong road ultimately ends in destruction in some form.

2. When in a situation where moral or behavioral choices are to be made, ask yourself, if your actions became public, would Jesus be lifted high? Asked another way, if your mother, father, brother, sister, son or daughter were with you at that moment how would you behave?

3. Be truthful. Don't operate in the dark. Nothing good ever comes from things that are secretive, suspicious or shrouded in darkness. Live in the light.

4. Faithfulness is a key attribute to the Christian faith. When you say you are going to do something, do it as promised. Live to your word. If you cannot live to your word through some circumstance, confirm that was your word, apologize for not living up to it

and ask for grace, doing your best to make amends for your failure.

5. Prioritize your faith and family above your job.

6. If people work for you or with you, make sure they know they are important, not just to the company, but more importantly, to you.

7. Give a good effort every day. Few things undermine our credibility as leaders of the faith faster than not putting forth an honest day's work. At the same time, if you are working without ceasing, ignoring faith, family and friends, you have a problem. A serious problem that will catch up to you. The path of a workaholic is misery and an inability to fully exhibit the fruits of the Spirit

8. Give each day to The Lord. Begin each workday with a prayer of thanksgiving to The Lord for your opportunity to serve Him and ask for his strength throughout the day. Take concerns to Him in prayer during the Day. Be thankful for the day, no matter what junk the world may present you with.

9. Seek for others around you to be successful. This seems counterintuitive, if you are career oriented. However, if those around you are successful following their interaction with you, it will likely reflect on you, and you will be showing people the good in you that comes from The Lord.

Scott McGregor

10. Above all, remember, that you are not defined by your job. You are defined by what you are as a person. For Christians and Non-Christians this means that your value is infinitely greater than what you do.

At the end of one's career they are likely to ask themselves, what was my work life about? Even further they will, as they become even more seasoned in life, ask what is my legacy? By exhibiting the Fruits of the Spirit in your work life and giving the credit to God, it will go a long way towards achieving the chief end of man, to glorify God, and hopefully avoid the meaninglessness of life that King Solomon suffered.

Will you always be able to follow these suggestions and show the Fruit of the Spirit? In my experience NO! We are human, prone to wander and there will be times when you fall short. That is not only likely to happen, but you can count on it. You are not called to be perfect; because we cannot be perfect by ourselves. You are called to rely on His grace when you stumble, repent (*turn around*) from any behavior falling short, ask His forgiveness and move forward. We are all on a path and there will be stumbles along the way. That's OK. Don't give up, the journey to glorifying God can be very trying, but I promise you it is worth every painful AND JOYFUL step!

222

The Question we asked at the beginning of this chapter was:

"How does success work as a Christian in a secular business world?

I hope you have come to a couple of answers to this question or are at least leaning that way. I would summarize the answer through the following statement. Success is an opportunity to lift the Lord Jesus Christ as Lord and Savior and give all Glory to Him. That is how one achieves real success works in the business world. You may not always be able to use the words of the faith to proclaim His Glory, but you sure can preach without using words.

At the end of the day it is absolutely possible to achieve success in the business world while exhibiting and growing in your faith. Just remember this one thing: it is not about you; it is all about Him.

Scott McGregor | Bio

Scott McGregor was born and raised in Rochester, NY. He has been blessed with a thirty-two year marriage to wife Lelia and has two beautiful daughters, Kerry and Kristin. Scott graduated from the University of North Carolina at Chapel Hill, Phi Beta Kappa with a Business of Science degree in Business Administration. He enjoyed a thirty-three year business career following college. Scott volunteers at his local church and is involved a variety of duties in the Evangelical Presbyterian Church.

CHAPTER XII

HE Is Who HE Says HE Is

By Ken Bitkowski

June 25, 2017

The day I gave my life to Christ.

So many times, in my 56 years; I've tried and failed, or should say imposed my will and not Gods will, to give my life to the Lord. But, after the death of my wife Beth (breast cancer) of 22 years; my life turned very dark very fast. I wanted to impose pain, the same pain I was feeling, among anyone who hurt her by the loss of my spouse. A phone call from the doctor's office by my wife's radiation oncology nurse (Marie) changed my life forever.

After numerous phone conversations I could not shake the darkness until she asked this one specific question *"Kenny do you want to live or die? If you chose to live then live through Jesus Christ our Lord. If you chose to die then Satan wins"*. All of sudden I felt the hole in my heart begin to heal. Palm Sunday she offered me to go to church; or as I speak of it today, service. As we entered Christian Center Church (Belle Vernon, Pa) I felt this spirit go straight through me and immediately turned to her and said; *"This is where God wants me to be"*. Two months later I went into the water (baptism) and gave everything (left everything) that I have ever done at the bottom of the pool.

I WAS FINALLY FREE!

The beginning of my personal relationship with Christ has just begun

Jesus spoke in John 16:33

[33] "I have told you all of this so that you may have peace in me! Here on earth you will have many trials and sorrows. But take heart because I have overcome the world."

Not realizing what these words or how true these words speak out loud for what I am beginning to embark on - a journey that could only be orchestrated by God!

The water was so refreshing and freeing that to this day has been the greatest day of my life-finally I did something for me!

"Hey Bobby, make sure the trailer is hooked on with the chain.".

As I was completing a job my phone rang; it was my neighbor. (10/11/2017) Nine months to the day that my wife passed. Nine long months since my wife passed and working on my personal relationship with Christ: reading my bible, reading scriptures and trying to understand how someone can love me and accept me with all that I have done. **My house was on fire!** Arriving home 25 minutes after the call (it should have taken 45 minutes). The realty of this loss complete loss, all my memories of my wife & my sons and how we took this condemned property and made it a home, now all was gone...

I broke down sobbing, crying; angry how can this happen- Why? Why God? Why? I called my son's, my family, brothers, sister's and Marie, along with my pastors -Pastor Tim and Pastor Mike - and we started to pray.

As everyone started to arrive the most amazing feeling of Peace came over me and then I heard His voice! *"Be still and know that I am God."* My focus changed, the tears stopped and my thought process was *"God please do not let any of these men or woman be injured or die trying to save 'Your' house"*. That's right *His* house. I realized God gave me the ability to be the carpenter that I was, the financial means, the memories he gave me - He knew that it was going to happen. It was written long before I entered His World.

The loss hit me hard. All the memories, all the sweat, blood and tears in renovating our home, was devastating but the overwhelming Peace that came upon me was a great joy that I knew that I was blessed. Blessed that no one loss there life, blessed that my FATHER was speaking to me, but most importantly blessed that I was listening to Him with the reassurance that HIS

WILL, and not mine, WAS taking place at that very moment in place and time. He knew that I would go through this! This was the beginning of complete and utter TRUST in what his Words were meant to be!

Proverbs 3:5

⁵ *"Trust in the Lord with all your heart and don't lean on YOUR understanding"*

FEELS LIKE I AM GETTING A COLD

November 6, 2017

After watching my home being dismantled, working, and praising OUR LORD AND SAVIOR, I awaken with a lump the right side of my neck, tender but I was moving forward and just like almost everyone of my generation was self-diagnosing. I was dealing with the insurance company, working, thanking our Father for all He has done for me, thanking Him for this trail that I am enduring and trusting Him was a normal day, so I thought. After returning home and ending my day with His Word, I noticed now that the lump was on both sides of my neck. No big deal - take a few Motrin, go to sleep, wake up I will feel better. When I awakened the lumps now multiplied under my left arm, clavicle areas, and groin. They were so profound. I looked like my body had aliens growing inside of me. The look on Maries face was nothing but utter fear. She immediately contacted Dr. B, the radiation oncology doctor that took care of my wife.

November 9, 2017

I arrived at the office to see Dr B, and the peace and calmness that I was experiencing was the true love of my Father, I did not fear, was not worried, and even to the point of complete and utter trust. All that kept going through my mind was; "*I am a child of the Most High*". After the examination and the concerned look on his face he immediately called Dr S, and within an hour I was in his office getting blood drawn, emergency CT scan, and an emergency PET scan. Something was going on, but I was at peace!!

November 10, 2017

After waking at my usual time 4:30 am and spending my time with the Father in worship, praising and reading the day readings, I watched ESPN. I was a diehard Steeler fan. I shut the TV off and leave for my appointment with Dr. S.

I arrived at the doctors for an 8:00 am appointment. After sitting in the room, which seemed like an eternity when in all actuality it was 10 min. The door opens and he comes in with an entourage. I am smiling and they ask how I am feeling today. I say *BLESSED, I AM BLESSED!* The news *"well my friend, you have a very aggressive form of lymphoma, large T cell lymphoma"*. The color just left Maries face. I look at them and ask what is the game plan? The Dr's assistant spoke and said, *"I am sorry Ken but you have a less than 10%; it's stage 5 and rapidly spreading"*. We recommend you follow up with hospice. WHAT? HOSPICE IS NOT AN OPTION! You said I have less than 10 %. I will take those odds because GOD did not put an expiration date on me. He is the One to decide my faith, not what these test say. His blood runs through me!

So the plan began!

Upon hearing this news, the Peace I have is undeniably God! All I keep hearing was *"I am who I say I am!"* He was not going to put my sons thru the death of their father so close to losing their mother. I knew that OUR GOD is not an angry God but a LOVING GOD!

If we want to receive the glory of our LORD, we must also share in suffering.

Arriving home I was at Peace but I had to let my sons, my family and my nephews know. I turned the TV on and was walking out the room when I noticed Pat Robertson was on; how strange I thought. I know I was watching ESPN. I went to the kitchen turned that one on-the same thing! Something drew me to him. Pat was praying at the end of the show looked directly in the TV and said; *"You, the man with the lumps in his neck, I want you to put your hands around your neck and pray this prayer rebuking the disease that has taken over your body!"* So, I did. I was so in tuned with what he was saying. Then I was trying to comprehend what just happen. Then I felt an overwhelming presence of GOD, His Grace and Mercy. I knew that HE LOVED ME. He came after me and I did not go after Him! I was His child.

Monday November 13, 2017

Admission day; test, port placement, echo and Chemo today at 3. Busy day. It's 3 pm and the treatment commences. The treatment was an aggressive type because it was the max treatment for my cancer-3 days in a row the Chemo and fluid day 4 each day was 6-8 hours; then off 2 weeks. During this time I continued to work, putting in windows, doors and bathroom. And all in all, my customers were blessing me with the love and compassion that a true Christ follower does. They were kind, compassionate and very appreciative that I was not only fighting for my life, but I was still fulfilling my contracts with them.

Tuesday November 14, 2017

Upon waking and showering I thought my mind was playing a trick on me; it felt as the lymph nodes were shrinking. "*I thought that it was only one treatment; how can that be?*"

I finished my routine at about 7:45 am and Dr. S & His PA arrived. I turned and the surprised look on their faces was that after the one treatment the lymph nodes were melting away. This was such a God thing that the look in both of their eyes was utter joy and they both were starting to really believe. It was such an awesome presence from the Holy Spirit.

Now the fight was on! The Peace I was feeling was undeniably GOD. He did say; "*I AM who I say I AM.*" Buckle up buttercup; we are in for a fight. Now the goal was 6 months chemo and fluids with a PET scan after 3rd treatment.

The second and third chemo were pretty much the same - some fatigue the normal chemo stuff. I go for my PET scan the morning my chemo was due. So when I walked in as I normally do, smiling and saying I am Blessed, I saw Dr. S' nurse and told her to check the scan instead of waiting until tomorrow. I am hooked up with cocktail that was prescribed - head laid back and was thanking God and praising Him. I closed my eyes and fell asleep for about 30 minutes. I opened my eyes and I felt the presence of the Lord. The team was walking towards me. I think, O crap this cannot be good! FATHER YOU ARE MY ROCK. The head nurse was leading the pack; following behind was the whole team - tears were running out of their eyes. I approached them and said I will be okay MY FATHER HAS DECIDED THIS, and they all said YES HE HAS. My scan WAS CLEAN - CANCER FREE!!! I broke down, cried and praised Him. I called everyone. There was such joy in everyone's voices. I finished my treatment for the day and flew home. I was so focused and feeling His Presence. I'll be going to see the Dr. tomorrow with the game plan.

It was a rough evening with the chemo side effects, but I knew that *"The Blood of Jesus run through me!"* I arrived at the office got plugged in and prayed for people. The Dr came over and states *"my friend"* he says, *"great news on the scan, if you want you can stop after this treatment or we can continue the course as we planned?"* Without hesitation I spoke *"WE STAY THE COURSE"* My Father wanted me to continue to trust Him, so I did!

After my 5th treatment I noticed blood in my stool; so I told my team. Needless to say, I was immediately admitted. My blood count was low; I was fatigued and needed two pints of blood. Also, a small cancer spot on my stomach was coming back. The spot was not anywhere as severe as the beginning but we chose to be aggressive so I began a 25-radiation treatment along with the chemo. I have 3 more chemo's and plugging through!

During this last couple of treatments I was totally beat up-weight was down, muscle mass lost. I knew my body would go through this. The cancer was gone and the chemo was now destroying all of my good cells. But my brother, *"Jesus Christ's blood runs through me!"* is all I could think of!

During those last 2 treatments, I was totally knocked out the box - no stamina, chronic fatigue. I was not able to work. My personal relationship with Christ was growing and growing every second. During my last few treatments, Marie, the person that was supposed to run with me through this trying time, choose to turn away and leave. God again knew this. As I look back God showed me all of this. He took me to Proverbs 5. This was the beginning of forgiveness. I spoke forgiveness!

Once my energy increased, I took off and began to get back to work: metal roof, rubber roof, pavilion, conversion on a Pizza Hut, and a pawnshop. This was a crazy 6 months out of treatments. Everyone is blessed and God is great. Coming up on my 6 month scan, I was living for Gods Word, worshipping, praising Him and gathering more strength from my Father. I go get my PET scan-the excitement is building. I go see the Dr. and the news was that there was a spot on my brain the size of a dime and then I spoke; *"Father you got me through the first battle, I know Your Son's blood through me"*. He will guide and lead me!

Game plan: three small therapy sessions and that should be it! After the first treatment as God promised; *"He is who He says He is"*. The shrinkage of the small spot was taking place. Two weeks after treatment with a positive CT result the area was already down nearly half the size. Three weeks later the second treatment had a positive result from another scan. It was gone but we completed the third treatment. That was when I totally realize that what I was speaking from the Word of God, that *His blood runs through me.*

During these last 13 months it wasn't always easy. My love for the Lord was growing, but I still was missing something and I did not know what it was. Then a conversation with my Christian brother brought light that I really did not forgive the person that walked away from me when I was in the battle; something to ponder. That evening I was reading the Word when I realized what God wanted me to do. That was to forgive from my heart! Not just speak it as I previously mentioned. That night I gave the forgiveness from my heart to the Lord. The freedom that was given to me was the greatest that I felt in a long time, that's when I learned to forgive from my heart – and, not just speak the words.

My anniversary for my original diagnosis was approaching and my PET scan was ordered. I was feeling on top of the world: working, praising, and worshipping. My Father was working in me and through me. The joy I was experiencing was overwhelming. The walk I was experiencing was tremendous.

March 16, 2019

The day of my scan was pretty uneventful; I arrived at 7:00 am being blessed by my Lord and Savior. I run through the test; get home to relax after a grueling week of work so I can get focused for service tomorrow.

March 17, 2019

After preforming my duties as head usher and hearing the word from our Pastor (intense and on point). I was standing near the exit greeting people as they left when our God makes His presence known. A young lady was standing in the back of the church (young meaning younger than me). Marisa how are you doing? Marisa was going through a difficult tie in her life. She smiled and we started talking when all of a sudden she looks at me and said; "*Who are you? What do you do? Do you have a past?*" A lot of questions I thought, but I smiled and said to her "*Boy do I have a past, but I am blessed.*" Her reply was "*would you like to get a bite to eat?*" and immediately responded "*yes.*" We were like two school kids skipping out of the church, being blessed beyond belief.

The lunch was great, the conversation was intense; yet the peace of our Lord was upon us. Although we had to rush because she had to get back at the church for a woman engagement with other women from the church. We arrived at the church she got into the van, and I continued to walk home. While I was walking a strange powerful sense came over me, what just happened? I had lunch with such a God fearing and loving woman, not once did I ask for God to send me someone. Yet alone some one as beautiful as her! Not the physical beauty that she has, but what was truly inside of her God, the Son and Holy Spirit.

March 18, 2019

Being impatient as I am I contacted the Dr's office and talked with them about my results. They wanted me to come in. I left early from the job I was doing and headed over. Upon arriving and sitting in the room - the look on their faces was utter fear. Yet, I have NO FEAR! *"BE STILL AND KNOW THAT I AM GOD"* is all I heard.

Once again the news, cancer has returned - T cell lymphocytic leukemia. Chemo does not work and life expectancy was 7-9 months. Without hesitation I said do you not realize what GOD HAS DONE? We will put on our coats of armor and fight. What is the plan? Stem cell transplant and immunotherapy, so all the testing begin; bone marrow biopsy, blood work, scans. You name it. I went through it all. During this time our Father being the Almighty One that He is, was building my relationship with Marisa. For example, God woke me one morning with the idea that I should speak to Marisa about the 911 memorial in Somerset, PA. All day I was battling with Him about why I should say it and all day His voice was louder and louder. That evening I was spending time with Marisa; and the bond between us, the bond that God brought us together, so I decided to speak what God wants me to. So I did. The expression on her face and the tears in her eyes was undeniably God! She said J (as she calls me), *"when that happened a few day later my dad took me and my daughter to see the devastation, and we always wanted to go back, but he since passed away."*

I was shaking to my core with such belief that I not only heard God, but listened. I listened. Thank you Father. A few days later I was with Marisa again: praising, reading and enjoying our time together. When I was ready to leave, she turned to me and said *"I love you more today than yesterday"* – WHAT? What did you say? She thought she scared me, but that was not the reason. It was God verifying this is all His plan. Startled, I began to explain what just happened. You see, when she spoke those words; no one, but no one other than the Father Himself knows they were the last words that my wife spoke prior to her passing. We always, no matter what we went through; we always said it to each other. *"I love you more than yesterday."* No one but God knew that. That was our personal saying; He was now speaking through her to verify that *He is who He says He is* and that He brought this union together. He is ever so present! That was when we both knew that God was with us. April 22nd, the day of the PET scan, Marisa accompanied me. It was a great joy and feeling to have some one with me; she had my back through another bump in the road. Our Lord and Savior has always been with me, I was just so blinded by this world that I lost myself – now I was found!

Scan completed and still at utter peace. Marisa and I finished our weekend with dinner and another beautiful worship service praising Our Lord.

Monday arrives; I leave work listening to worship and my phone rings - it's the doctor's office they need me to come in for another PET scan. They were thinking that the IV contrast did not take so off I go for another test! I arrive for another PET scan and the atmosphere was definitely buzzing with something. It was joy; people smiling and helping others. This was all God! I complete the test and return to work. A little after lunch the doctor's office called and I can hear crying and others in the background praising God and crying. She had it on speaker, she said, *"Ken your scans are completely clear"*. Upon hearing this I immediately started to cry tears of joy. I had to tell Marisa so I left work to go to her place of work, upon arriving and asking for her, she comes out with a smile on her face. I grabbed her and I told her the news. We hugged and cried – My Fathers greatness has prevailed again! Until I saw the doctor I was not going to tell everyone (family nor friends).

Tuesday the day will forever be. We arrive at the doctors office go into the room. We were laughing, thanking Him and worshipping Him all the time we drove, 1 hour and 8 minutes, to this appointment. The doctors comes in, look at me and say; *"my friend, you are cancer free. There is no scientific explanation for this? No treatment! The PET scan showed no cancer. It is God that did this for you!"* We hugged and tears were in both of our eyes, but I saw the fire in his eyes about what GOD HAS DONE! *NOT ONCE, NOT TWICE, BUT A THIRD TIME!* Then it hit me hard. The Father sent the Holy Spirit-The Trinity. As we were leaving we met my entire team and the joy that they were experiencing with us, not only of the cancer being cleared, but also we announce that Marisa and I were getting married! Such a blessed moment in the mist of Our God! As I said earlier; first God healed me, then my relationship with Christ grew and He intervened the second time and I know the Father has sent the Holy Spirit to confirm *He is who He says He is*. As I some times refer to the Father, Son and Holy Spirit, the big three, the Trifecta was here alive in me and through me. Their presence has been shown not only to me, but to everyone that I came across during this Job moment that I was walking through!

Through this amazing and wonderful journey God has shown me so many things. He explained what He saw when I was first diagnosed and was healed I kept wondering why me, why not Beth or someone else and God spoke very clearly to me and said *"you trusted Me and you did not ask for a healing, you prayed for others and not yourself, you TRUSTED MY WORDS AND PROMISES"*. Then around Easter, which was my favorite time of the year because Jesus died for my sins and I always wondered how I would respond if I saw a miracle from God, God spoke to me at 3:00 am and said, *"so what are you going to do?"* For three days He did the same thing. I thought He wanted me to organize my day with work etc.

That was not the case.

I got up walked to the bathroom washed my face looked into the mirror and it hit me – I said *"Father I am a miracle"*. *"Yes"* He says, *"so what are you going to do?"*

I am Blessed!
Mathew 28:19

[19] *"Therefore go and make disciples of all nations, baptizing them in the name of The Father, and of The Son and the Holy Spirit"*

The beginning ....

Ken Bitkowski | Bio

Ken was born in a small town outside of Pittsburgh Pa; called Duquesne, he is the second child of 5 children.

Ken has owned his own construction company for nearly 30 years.

Prior to Ken's walk with Christ, he was incarcerated for 5 years. Upon entering his incarcerated time he was a devote catholic, and felt God put him there for a reason; but he had no clue what this reason could of been.

Currently he is active in his home, church as an usher, volunteers for celebrate recovery, reads, works, and planning for his future with fiancée, Marisa, and praising and worshiping His Lord and Savior!

Kenneth Bitkowski
103 Charity Lane
Belle Vernon, PA 15012
bitkowski@comcast.net

About John Westley Clayton

"You are who and what you
create yourself to be"
—John Westley Clayton

Rock Star Maker, Bestselling Author, Publisher of Bestselling Books, Sales Trainer, Leadership Trainer, Life Trainer, Life Mentor, Keynote Speaker... ROCK STAR!!!

John Westley Clayton is the publishing arm of the *Journeys To Success* series; and along with other multiple titles to the John

Westley Publishing brand, has come to represent quality within the industry.

Surviving a rough childhood, along with multiple setbacks, unbeknownst to John Westley, this fueled the fire for him to set out on his own and develop a pathway to success that fits his puritan work ethic. Through the years John Westley created a successful resume, outperforming in all areas of business, sales and management.

Through the years something started to awaken in him; only focusing on wealth development for years may have created physical comfort and freedom, but there was something missing. The pieces finally fell into place when he discovered *Think & Grow Rich* by Napoleon Hill.

Focusing on the prize of financial achievement alone wasn't enough; developing ones self as a well-rounded human being was the elusive secret John Westley had been looking for for many years.

John Westley began manifesting a new reality and became a Napoleon Hill Certified Instructor and part of The John Maxwell TEAM, helping others achieve their goals.

As the CEO & Founder of John Westley Enterprises, John Westley has become the '*Rock Star Maker*' and the secret weapon behind many of today's thought leaders. Under his *Rock Star 4 life* and Veritas Leadership Institute brand, he helps individuals build the life they want by stepping out of their comfort zone and onto a

b

bigger stage. Providing group coaching, one-on-one mentoring, image and personal brand creation and publishing.

For the past 10 years, he's been teaching entrepreneurs, educators, corporate leaders and people from all walks of life how to create the life they truly desire by making the choices that best serve them in their professional and personal lives.

Today, as a peak performance coach and leadership/personal development strategist and trainer, John Westley's programs have launched dozens of individuals into ROCK STAR status.

Got a dream? He'll place it center stage.

www.johnwestley.com

info@johnwestley.com

d

Made in the USA
Middletown, DE
09 September 2019